EYEWITNESS
MONEY

Ancient bronze coin of the city of Hatra, 3rd century BCE

Australian cupro-nickel 50 cents, 1970

Bolivian gold 8-scudos coin, 1841

Indian gold pagodas, 17th–19th century

Indian gold mohur, 17th century

Ceylon (Sri Lanka) 10-cent note, 1942

Djibouti French colonial note, 20th century

Ancient Roman medals showing minting (below) and banking (right)

Moroccan bronze coins, unseparated, as taken from the mould, 19th century

Ancient Greek silver coin showing Alexander the Great, 4th century BCE

Spanish silver "piece-of-eight" reales from Mexico, 1732

Gold 10-ducat coin of Transylvania, 17th century

EYEWITNESS
MONEY

Written by
JOE CRIBB

USSR cupro-nickel
ruble, 1967

Ancient Chinese
bronze hoe-shaped
coin, 6th century BCE

American gold
eagle, 1797

Siamese paper money, 1860s

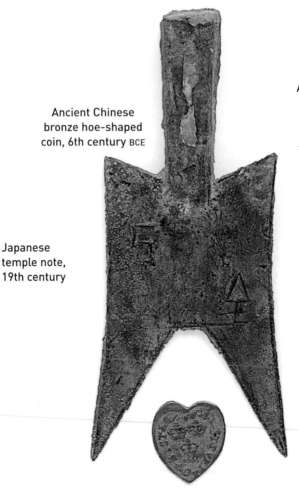

Japanese
temple note,
19th century

English brass
halfpenny
token, 1665

Zambian bronze
penny, 1966

English gold sovereign (1901) and
brass sovereign balance

Penguin
Random
House

Project editor Linda Martin
Art editor Richard Czapnik
Senior editor Sophie Mitchell
Senior art editor Julia Harris
Editorial director Sue Unstead
Art director Anne-Marie Bulat
Special photography Chas Howson, Department
of Coins and Medals, the British Museum

RELAUNCH EDITION

DK UK

Senior editor Francesca Baines
Senior art editor Spencer Holbrook
Jacket coordinator Claire Gell
Jacket designer Natalie Godwin
Jacket design development manager Sophia MTT
Producer, pre-production Jacqueline Street
Producer Vivienne Yong
Managing art editor Philip Letsu
Publisher Andrew Macintyre
Associate publishing director Liz Wheeler
Design director Stuart Jackman
Publishing director Jonathan Metcalf

DK INDIA

Assistant editor Ateendriya Gupta
Art editor Alpana Aditya
DTP designer Pawan Kumar
Senior DTP designer Harish Aggarwal
Picture researcher Sakshi Saluja
Jacket designer Surabhi Wadhwa
Managing jackets editor Saloni Singh
Pre-production manager Balwant Singh
Managing editor Kingshuk Ghoshal
Managing art editor Govind Mittal

This Eyewitness ® Guide has been conceived by
Dorling Kindersley Limited and Editions Gallimard

First published in Great Britain in 1990
This revised edition published in Great Britain in 2005, 2016
by Dorling Kindersley Limited,
80 Strand, London WC2R 0RL

A CIP catalogue record for this book is available from the British Library

ISBN: 978-0-2412-5889-7

Printed and bound in China

A WORLD OF IDEAS:
SEE ALL THERE IS TO KNOW

www.dk.com

Ancient Roman
silver coin,
3rd century BCE

Ancient Indian
gold coin,
1st century CE

Australian
aluminium-brass,
two-dollar
coin, 1998

Ottoman Turkish
gold zeri-mahbub,
18th century

Ancient Roman gold bar
made from melted-down
coins, 4th century

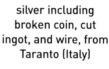

Ancient Greek
silver including
broken coin, cut
ingot, and wire, from
Taranto (Italy)

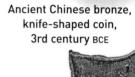

Ancient Chinese bronze,
knife-shaped coin,
3rd century BCE

Persian
silver
wire lairn
coin, 16th
century

Tonga
cupro-nickel
one-pa'anga
coin, 1977

Contents

Chinese silver good-luck
coin charm, 19th century

Indian cupro-nickel
10-paise coin, 1964

This is money

It is difficult to imagine a world without money; every country has its own, and its history reaches back to the earliest written records of human activity. For most people, money is coins, bank notes (bills), and plastic cards. But in the past, money has been feathers, stones, and shells. They are all money because they are an acceptable and recognized means of payment. Unseen money, like money stored in bank computer records, is also real money.

Everyday money
Bank notes, coins, and plastic cards come in many different forms, but they are all "money", used to make payments.

Early money

The oldest written records of money are from ancient Mesopotamia (now southern Iraq) about 4,500 years ago. Cuneiform (wedge-shaped writing) inscriptions describe payments in weighed amounts of silver. Weighed amounts of metal have been used ever since, leading to the invention of coins.

Goose weight
The ancient Mesopotamians made official [weights] to weigh silver accurately. This one [weighs 10] shekels, with 60 shekels in a mina.

Mesopotamian money
This tablet describes prices in the reign of Sin-Kasid of Uruk (1865–1804 BCE): "One shekel of silver on the local standard could buy three measures of barley, twelve mina of wool, ten mina of bronze, or three measures of sesame oil."

Hammurabi's laws
This big stone column shows a god giving Hammurabi, King of Babylonia (1792–1750 BCE), the laws referring to how silver should be used.

Ten

Twelve

Wool

Barley

Bronze

Cuneiform
Deciphering cuneiform script has helped us find other descriptions of money paid in weighed amounts of silver in ancient Mesopotamia. The characters above feature on the tablet's inscription.

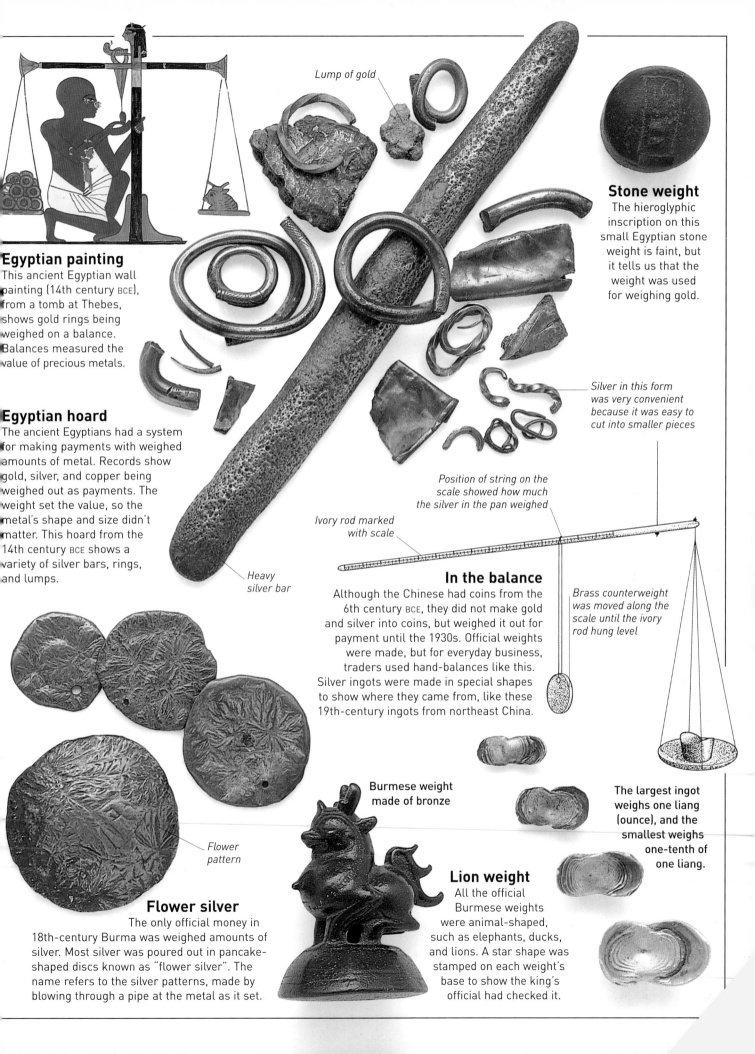

Egyptian painting

This ancient Egyptian wall painting (14th century BCE), from a tomb at Thebes, shows gold rings being weighed on a balance. Balances measured the value of precious metals.

Egyptian hoard

The ancient Egyptians had a system for making payments with weighed amounts of metal. Records show gold, silver, and copper being weighed out as payments. The weight set the value, so the metal's shape and size didn't matter. This hoard from the 14th century BCE shows a variety of silver bars, rings, and lumps.

Lump of gold

Heavy silver bar

Stone weight

The hieroglyphic inscription on this small Egyptian stone weight is faint, but it tells us that the weight was used for weighing gold.

Silver in this form was very convenient because it was easy to cut into smaller pieces

Position of string on the scale showed how much the silver in the pan weighed

Ivory rod marked with scale

In the balance

Although the Chinese had coins from the 6th century BCE, they did not make gold and silver into coins, but weighed it out for payment until the 1930s. Official weights were made, but for everyday business, traders used hand-balances like this. Silver ingots were made in special shapes to show where they came from, like these 19th-century ingots from northeast China.

Brass counterweight was moved along the scale until the ivory rod hung level

Flower pattern

Burmese weight made of bronze

The largest ingot weighs one liang (ounce), and the smallest weighs one-tenth of one liang.

Flower silver

The only official money in 18th-century Burma was weighed amounts of silver. Most silver was poured out in pancake-shaped discs known as "flower silver". The name refers to the silver patterns, made by blowing through a pipe at the metal as it set.

Lion weight

All the official Burmese weights were animal-shaped, such as elephants, ducks, and lions. A star shape was stamped on each weight's base to show the king's official had checked it.

Funny money?

As heavy as stone, as light as a feather, money comes in many forms. In some tribal societies, payments were made with objects of a recognized value: ornaments such as shells, tools such as hoes, and foodstuffs such as salt. As with our money today, tribal societies had strict rules about the value and payment of their money; it was used to settle social obligations such as marriage payments, compensation, and fines.

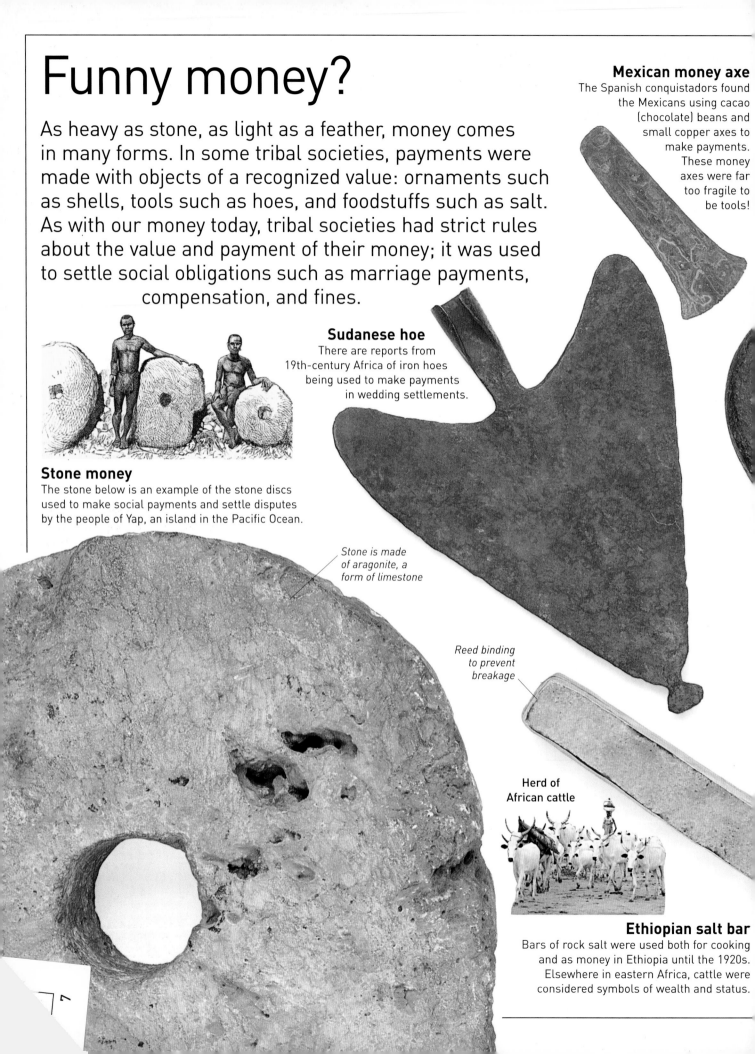

Mexican money axe
The Spanish conquistadors found the Mexicans using cacao (chocolate) beans and small copper axes to make payments. These money axes were far too fragile to be tools!

Sudanese hoe
There are reports from 19th-century Africa of iron hoes being used to make payments in wedding settlements.

Stone money
The stone below is an example of the stone discs used to make social payments and settle disputes by the people of Yap, an island in the Pacific Ocean.

Stone is made of aragonite, a form of limestone

Reed binding to prevent breakage

Herd of African cattle

Ethiopian salt bar
Bars of rock salt were used both for cooking and as money in Ethiopia until the 1920s. Elsewhere in eastern Africa, cattle were considered symbols of wealth and status.

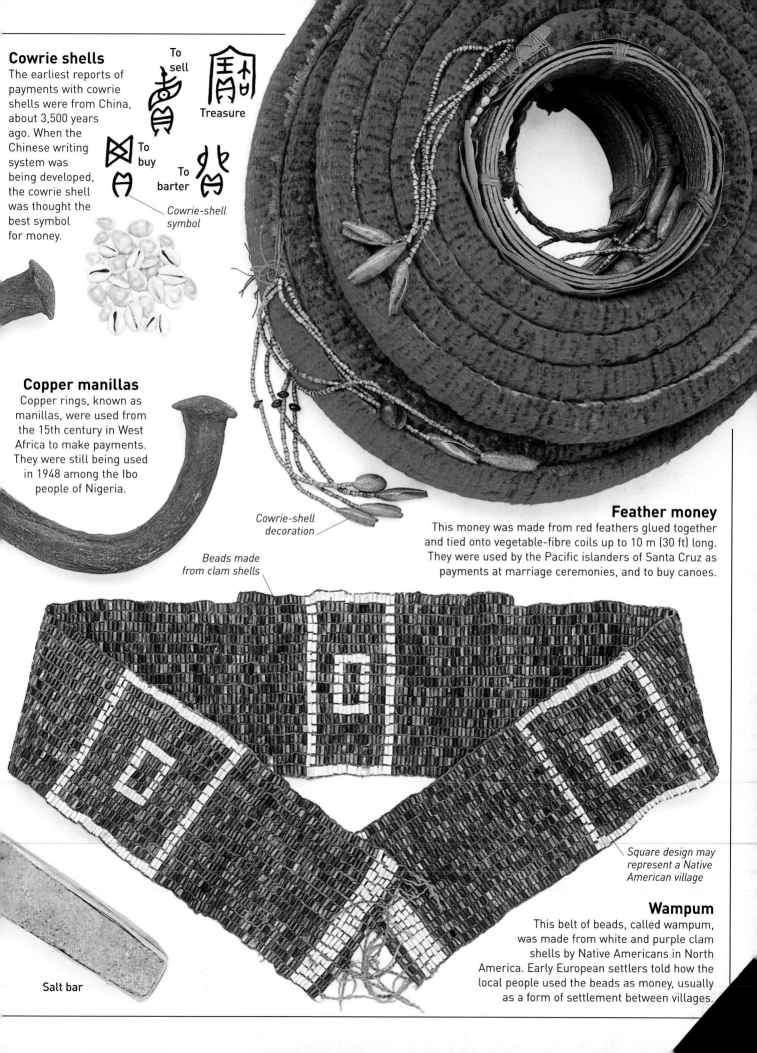

Cowrie shells

The earliest reports of payments with cowrie shells were from China, about 3,500 years ago. When the Chinese writing system was being developed, the cowrie shell was thought the best symbol for money.

To sell

Treasure

To buy

To barter

Cowrie-shell symbol

Copper manillas

Copper rings, known as manillas, were used from the 15th century in West Africa to make payments. They were still being used in 1948 among the Ibo people of Nigeria.

Cowrie-shell decoration

Beads made from clam shells

Feather money

This money was made from red feathers glued together and tied onto vegetable-fibre coils up to 10 m (30 ft) long. They were used by the Pacific islanders of Santa Cruz as payments at marriage ceremonies, and to buy canoes.

Salt bar

Square design may represent a Native American village

Wampum

This belt of beads, called wampum, was made from white and purple clam shells by Native Americans in North America. Early European settlers told how the local people used the beads as money, usually as a form of settlement between villages.

The first coins

Coining tools
Roman coin showing ancient tools for making coins: punch (top), anvil (centre), hammer (right), and tongs (left).

Coins are metal pieces marked with a design to show they are money. The earliest-known coins were made in the 7th century BCE in the kingdom of Lydia (now Turkey). The Lydians used weighed lumps of electrum (a mixture of gold and silver) as money, and stamped them with pictures to confirm their weight and value. This stamping process is called "minting". The stamp was a seal to identify the person who had guaranteed the coin's weight – Lydian kings used a lion's head on their coins. This new way to organize money was a big success, and soon spread into Europe.

Mark made by punches

One-stater coins

¹⁄₆-stater coins

Lydian electrum coins
The weight of Lydian money was measured in "staters", about 14 g (½ oz) each. Fractional coins were also made, including coins as small as ¹⁄₉₆ stater. Each metal lump was placed on an anvil, and the punches were pushed into the lump with a hammer. The anvil was engraved with the lion's-head emblem of the Lydian kings, so this image was stamped onto these coins (600 BCE).

¹⁄₂₄-stater coin

Greek letters

Personal seals
The Greek letters on this Turkish coin (above) mean "I am the seal of Phanes". This Greek seal names its owner, Mandronax.

Caria, c.530 BCE

Andros, c.525 BCE

Ceos, c.525 BCE

Marked ingot made of copper

Aegina, c.540 BCE   **Athens, c.540 BCE**

Early silver coins
The idea of coinage spread from western Turkey into the Greek world. The pictures on four of these coins were the emblems of the place of issue: a lion for Caria in Turkey; a vase, a squid, and a turtle for the Aegean islands. The beetle is the emblem of an Athenian official. These coins were goddess Artemis (right) at emple, Turkey, in 560 BCE.

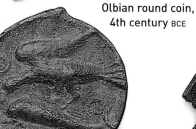

Knife-shaped coin

Olbian dolphin coins, 4th century BCE

Hoe-shaped coin

Olbian round coin, 4th century BCE

Cowrie-shell shaped coin

Copper coins

Before coinage was adopted in Olbia in Russia, in Rome and other Latin and Etruscan (pre-Roman) cities of Italy, weighed pieces of cast copper were used as money. Under the influence of Greek coins, designs were added to these copper ingots (pieces of cast metal made in a mould) to turn them into coins.

Chinese coins

The earliest Chinese coins (about 500 BCE) were made from bronze in the shape of the tools and cowrie shells that the Chinese had previously used as money.

Elephant-sized coin!

In Rome, early marked ingots kept the rectangular shape used before for unmarked ingots. This Indian elephant (below) refers to the war elephants of a Greek army that invaded southern Italy in 280 BCE.

Shogun

Shoguns were military dictators who ruled Japan from the 12th to the 19th century.

Thai ring-coins

Before coins, the people of Thailand used weighed silver rings as money. When rings were made into coins (17th century), their shape was changed by bending or hammering.

Gold coin, 1601

Japanese ingot coins

In the late 16th century, the Japanese leader Ieyasu, who became the first Tokugawa Shogun, reorganized Japan's monetary system. His coins were hammered or cast slabs, like the ingots used before.

Silver coin, 1601

Gold coin, 1818

The first paper money

Bank notes are only pieces of paper, but what they represent is valuable. The Chinese were the first to handle money as printed paper documents. In the 10th century, the Chinese government issued heavy iron coins with little value. People left these coins with merchants and used handwritten receipts instead. By the 11th century, the government printed receipts as official money.

Difficult to lose!
This bank note (left) was big to carry, but the largest ever was 22.8 x 33 cm (9 x 13 in).

Japanese note
Paper money spread to Japan in the 17th century. Most notes were issued by feudal clans and temples.

Japanese "bookmark" note of 1746

Temple money
Japanese temples, like this one in Kyoto, acted like banks, issuing their own paper money.

Chinese paper money
In the centre of the design of this 14th-century Chinese note you can just see the ??? it represented. ??? would have ??? bout 3.5 kg (8 lb).

English money order
Before official printed bank notes appeared in Europe, handwritten paper money was in use. This note from 1665 asked for 50 pounds of money to be paid to a servant.

Swedish bank note

In 1661, during a time of shortage of silver coins, the Swedish Stockholm Bank began to issue Europe's first printed paper money. This note from 1666 (left) represented 100 dalers.

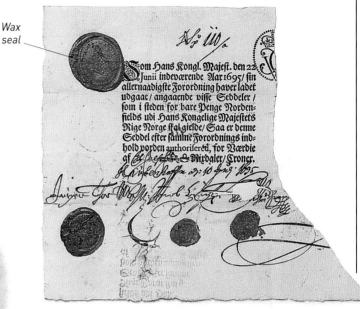

Wax seal

John Law

The Scotsman John Law was responsible for the issue of paper money in France.

Norwegian merchant's note

Following the Swedish example, a Norwegian merchant, Jorgen Thor Mohlen, issued printed notes for circulation as money in 1695.

French Royal bank note

Scotsman John Law brought printed paper money to France. In 1718, the Paris bank he set up received the French king's approval to issue notes valued in silver coin (left). With too many notes issued, they became worthless.

Bank of Scotland note

During the late 17th century, printed paper money began to be issued in Britain. The Bank of Scotland issued notes valued in Scottish money, like this one dated 1723 (above). Twelve Scottish pounds were equal to one English pound.

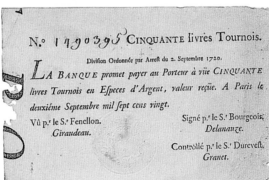

Italian Papal note

This 31-scudi note (left) from the Bank of the Holy Spirit in Rome was issued in 1786, in the reign of Pope Pius VI, for circulation in the Papal States. This was Europe's first national bank.

New Jersey bill

As the British government didn't give coins to its North American colonies, they issued their own paper "bills" (above).

Commercial bank note

Commercial banks have promoted paper money. This note (right) was issued in 1954 in Hong Kong by the Chartered Bank, a London bank with global branches.

How coins are made

A coin is made by marking a piece of metal with designs – a process called "minting". Designs are stamped onto the metal by pressing it between two metal tools, called dies. This basic coin-making method was invented 2,600 years ago, using an anvil and punch as dies. Today's dies are part of a large, electrically powered machine press.

Millennium Crown design by Jeffery Matthews

Pure copper ingot

Plaster model
Before a coin is made, an artist creates a design. Once the design is approved, it is engraved by hand on a plaster model. Complex designs make it hard for forgers to copy them.

Pellets of pure nickel

Cupro-nickel alloy is cast in a slab, ready to be rolled to the thickness of the coin

Time is measured from the Greenwich Meridian, London

Recording the design
Once the plaster model is finalized, a computer records every detail of the surface. A ruby-tipped tracer carefully traces the design in a process that lasts about 20 hours.

Making cupro-nickel
The Millennium Crown is made from an alloy called cupro-nickel. This alloy is made by mixing together pure copper and nickel. Cupro-nickel is often used to make high-denomination coins because it looks like the silver used in the past to make coins.

Raised version of the design — **Master punch**

"Incuse", or punched, version of the design in reverse — **Matrix**

Working punch

Working die

Checking the design
After the computer has traced the design, the recorded details are checked on screen for accuracy.

Cutting the master punch
The computer record is used to direct an engraving machine that cuts the coin-sized master punch.

Minting tools
A single master punch is used so that all the coins are identical. It stamps the design onto the matrix, which, in turn, stamps several working punches. Hundreds of working dies, which will be used to strike the coins, are then made from the working punches.

"What's Past is Prologue" from The Tempest by William Shakespeare

Edge-lettering tool
The Millennium Crown has lettering on its edge. These strips are used to impress the inscription onto the coin.

Making blanks
Once the cupro-nickel strip has been rolled out to the correct thickness, it is passed through a press that stamps the blank coins or "blanks" out of it. The remaining strip, called "scissel", is melted down and used to make more strips.

Coining press
The blank is placed in the coining press, into which the working dies for the front and back of the coin have been fitted. It is then squashed between these dies.

Clockface at midnight, New Year's Eve, 1999, for the start of the new Millennium

Once the blanks have been cut, the strip is called "scissel"

Fresh-cut blanks

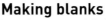

Coin-shaped metal blanks are cut out by a blanking press and then passed through a machine to give them a slightly raised rim

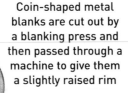

Rimmed blanks

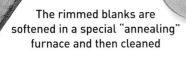

The rimmed blanks are softened in a special "annealing" furnace and then cleaned

Back (reverse)

Front (obverse)

The end result
The Millennium Crown has a face value of five pounds and was made by the British Royal Mint to mark the end of the Second Millennium.

Bank notes

Making bank notes is a secret, complex business. Printers must ensure that notes are impossible for forgers to copy easily. The world's busiest bank note printers make specimen notes to show customers its techniques. There are four stages: design, papermaking, ink-mixing, and printing.

Computer design
After an artist has created a bank note design, it is perfected on screen using a computer program. Colour sample proofs are printed for approval. With the design finalized, the different printings are separated on a computer before the lithography printing plates are made.

Engraver at work
The engraver takes weeks to hand-cut design details onto a steel plate.

Sharp engraving tools, called burins, are used for cutting the design into the plate

A burnisher is used for smoothing the flat surface

Magnifying glass
The engraver needs a magnifying glass to work on the tiny details of the design that make it hard for a forger to copy the note.

Reflecting green   *Reflecting red*

Paper quality
Notes are printed on paper made from cotton fibres. Only quality paper can take the daily wear and tear. It often has security thread to deter forgery.

Top security
Plastic thread in the paper cannot be photocopied as its colour varies from red to green under light. When photocopied, it simply looks black.

Intaglio printing plate
The design of most bank notes is usually printed using a design that has been hand-engraved on a steel plate. This one shows Thomas de la Rue, founder of De La Rue, the bank note printers.

Intaglio proof
When the intaglio plate is inked, the ink fills the engraved design. The plate is printed under high pressure onto the paper, raising an inked impression of the design. Some banks use this to add identification marks for people with limited vision.

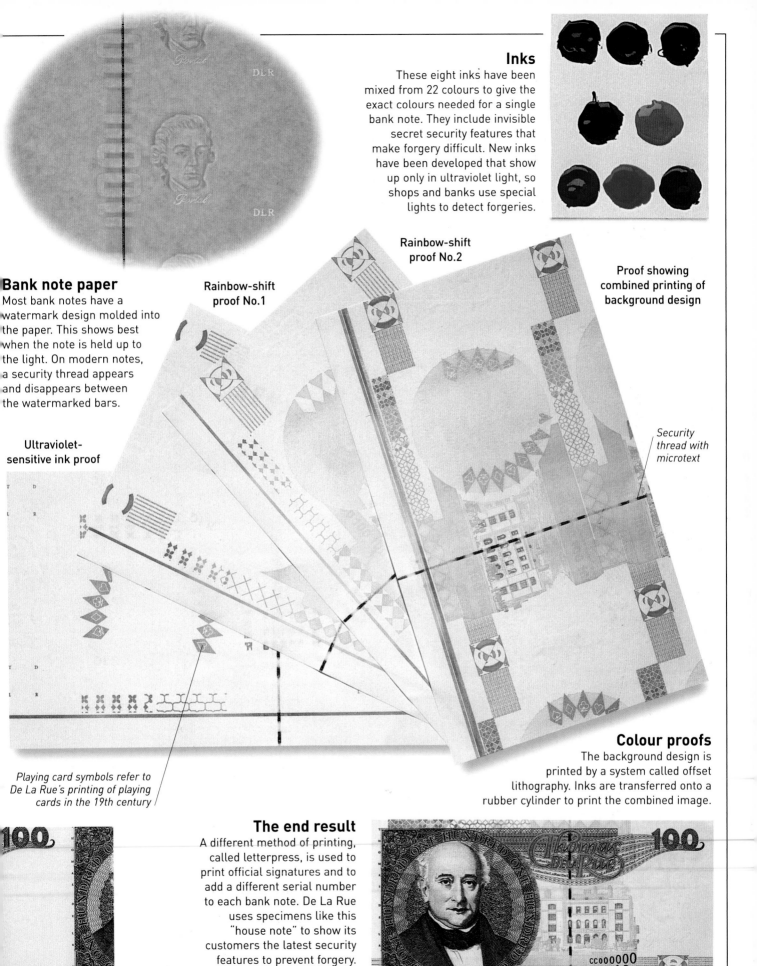

Inks

These eight inks have been mixed from 22 colours to give the exact colours needed for a single bank note. They include invisible secret security features that make forgery difficult. New inks have been developed that show up only in ultraviolet light, so shops and banks use special lights to detect forgeries.

Bank note paper

Most bank notes have a watermark design molded into the paper. This shows best when the note is held up to the light. On modern notes, a security thread appears and disappears between the watermarked bars.

Rainbow-shift proof No.1

Rainbow-shift proof No.2

Proof showing combined printing of background design

Security thread with microtext

Ultraviolet-sensitive ink proof

Playing card symbols refer to De La Rue's printing of playing cards in the 19th century

Colour proofs

The background design is printed by a system called offset lithography. Inks are transferred onto a rubber cylinder to print the combined image.

The end result

A different method of printing, called letterpress, is used to print official signatures and to add a different serial number to each bank note. De La Rue uses specimens like this "house note" to show its customers the latest security features to prevent forgery. They are demonstrated to banks all over the world.

Forgeries and fakes

Forgery, the art of making false money, is a serious crime. In the past, punishments for forgery included being deported and being executed. Driven by the profit to be made by turning inexpensive pieces of metal or paper into something of value, forgers continue to break the law. Today's punishments are large fines or imprisonment. Despite the devices adopted by coinmakers and bank-note printers to make forgeries difficult, plenty of forgers still take risks.

Imprisonment is the most common punishment for forgers caught in the act today, but heavy fines can be imposed

Plated forgeries
These copies of gold Greek coins were made from gold-plated copper. They were recognized as forgeries when the plating cracked to reveal green copper beneath.

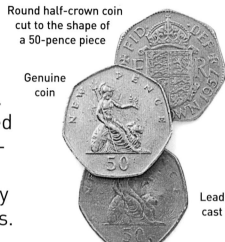

Round half-crown coin cut to the shape of a 50-pence piece

Genuine coin

Lead cast

Copies
These two copies of a British 50-pence were meant to deceive those not familiar with the new coin.

Silver case

Tin disc

Non-existent bank

Tin dollar
This Chinese forgery of a Mexican silver dollar, found in Shanghai in the 1930s, was made by enclosing a tin disc in a silver case.

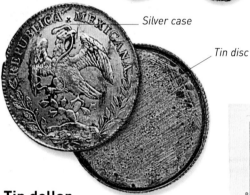

Non-existent bank
Italy was short of small change in the 1970s, so some banks made small-change notes. A forger printed his own notes, but the bank name didn't exist!

Hand-drawn forgery
All the details on this false Swedish 10-daler bank note of 1868 were copied by hand. This forgery took a long time!

Spot the difference

The first note is a forgery of the 1835 Bank of Rome note on the far right (both reduced in size). The forger copied most of the details (including the words at the bottom that say "the law punishes forgers"), but his mistakes enabled his crime to be detected. How many can you spot?

The hangman's noose

This cartoon takes the form of a Bank of England note, and criticizes the severe punishment for using forged notes. The pound sign is a hangman's noose.

Checking change

To protect against forged coins or notes, traders carefully check all the money paid to them. When money was gold and silver coins, the best precaution was to check that the gold or silver was of good quality, and that each coin contained the full weight of precious metal.

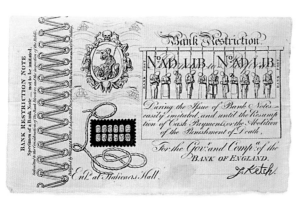

Greek silver coin, 5th century

Punch to test if coin was plated

Portuguese Indian coin, 1688

Checked coins

To ensure a coin was not plated, traders cut into the surface, as with this Greek coin. The Indian coin has been checked with small engraved punches.

24-carat gold coin

Touchstone

To check the quality of a gold coin, a trader would mark the black touchstone with the equivalent gold carat touch needle (above), and then compare that mark with the mark the coin left.

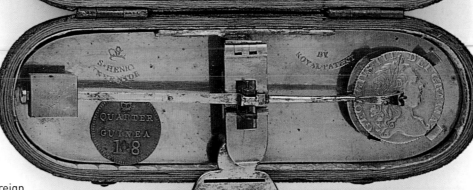

Balance and weights

This British balance scale (right) was used in the 18th century to weigh gold coins. The brass weights (above) are from 17th-century Belgium and are varied, so that foreign gold coins imported from other countries could be weighed.

A plated coin of the correct weight is too thick to go through this slot

19

Money and trade

Money is at the centre of trade, whether in a local store or on the international commodities (products) market. Money, the "medium of exchange", enables both buyer and seller to agree to part with what they have to get what they want. In the past, money was precious metals, so trade ships carried chests of coins. Today, money rarely moves in trade. Most international payments are made by telephone and computer.

Silver owls
The silver coins of Athens were called "owls" because their design included Little Owl, the bird of the goddess Athena. The design was so popular that many countries issued similar coins, as seen on this map.

Turkey

Iraq

Italy

Iran

Palestine

Athens

Egypt

Southern Arabia

Dutch traders' manual
In the 16th century, so many foreign coins were handled by Dutch merchants that they used handbooks to identify current coins from other lands and indicate their value. This one shows Scandinavian silver dalers.

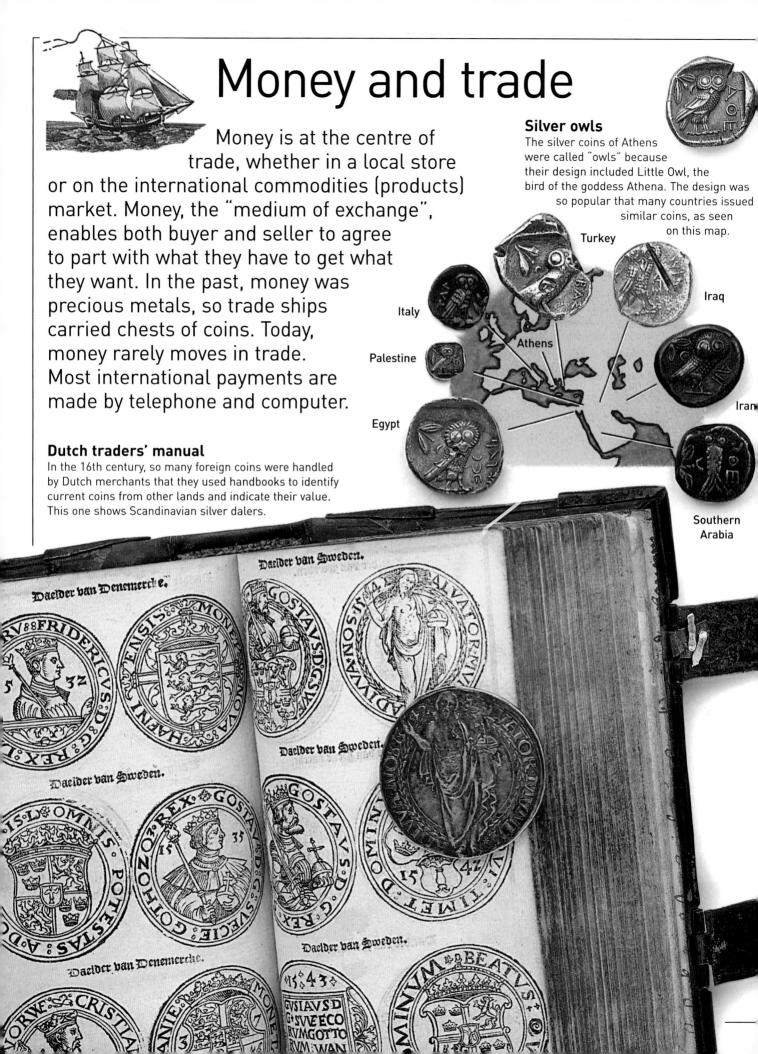

Daelder van Denemercke.

Daelder van Sweden.

Daelder van Sweden.

Daelder van Sweden.

Daelder van Sweden.

Daelder van Denemercke.

Canada

Australia

Great Britain

Barter

Today, international trade is often carried out without money; tractors are swapped for jam, and grain for oil. This form of trade, known as "barter", has a long history; the earliest record of it comes from ancient Egypt, 4,500 years ago. The problem with barter is deciding how many pots of jam each tractor is worth.

West Indies

Pieces of eight

Spanish silver "pieces of eight" (8-reales coins) were popularly known as "dollars". The Spanish empire exported so many of these in trade that they were adopted in many countries as official money, but stamped or cut for local use. These coins are from the Spanish mint in Mexico City.

British West Africa

China

Dollar note

At the end of Spanish rule in the Americas, the new republics, including Mexico, continued to issue dollars for export to China. This Mexican dollar note was printed for a British trade bank to issue in China.

Chinese gold bar

Gold bars

Spanish silver pieces of eight were traded with China in exchange for gold. Gold bars like this were shipped back to Europe, where they were made into coins. This bar was found in the wreck of a merchant ship sailing from China to Europe.

Bill of exchange

Coins are no longer used in global trade, as money is usually paid by messages between bank computers or by written instructions like this bill of exchange. A bill of exchange is a written order signed by a trader instructing a second person, or bank, to pay an amount in a specific currency to another trader by a specific date.

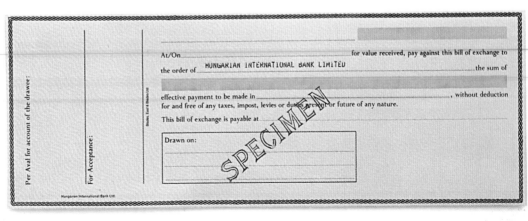

Money in war

Throughout history, money and war have marched hand in hand. Money pays for the arms and services of mercenaries – soldiers who will fight for any country that pays enough. The hardships of war have led to new forms of money in cities under siege, as well as by governments that have run out of money. Too often money provides the reward for success in war. Soldiers have often been recruited on the understanding that they would be paid from the enemy's booty.

Alexander the Great
This silver coin was made in 326 BCE to commemorate Alexander the Great's victory over an Indian king.

Siege!
In the siege of Athens by the Spartans in 406 BCE, silver owl coins ran out, so golden statues were melted to make coins.

Siege note
When a Prussian army besieged French revolutionary forces in the German city of Mainz, in 1793, the French army issued emergency notes (left) for use within the city.

During the English Civil War (1642–1648), the Cavaliers fought the Roundheads for control of the country

Charles I
England's King Charles I issued this coin (above) in 1644 at his Oxford mint.

Siege silver
In 1644, Cavaliers (royalist troops) besieged in Scarborough Castle cut up silver plates for coins. The castle and denomination were stamped on them.

War notes
In the American Civil War, the southern Confederate States financed the war by issuing notes to be repaid in coins two years after the war ended.

Confederate forces, flag flying, storm a Yankee-held fort during the American Civil War

Boer wars badges

These patriotic badges (below) show the British Commander-in-Chief, Lord Roberts, and his officer, Colonel Baden-Powell, who issued the Mafeking siege notes. Baden-Powell later founded the Boy Scout Movement.

Distortion by blow of bullet

Life savers!

In Europe's Thirty Years War (1618–1648), many Germans carried a St George thaler (top left), believing it would stop bullets. At the Battle of Culloden, Scotland, a soldier escaped death because this copper halfpenny deflected the bullet.

Boer coins

Boer wars money

Emergency issues of money were made by the Boers (Dutch settlers in South Africa) and the British in the Second Boer War in South Africa (1899–1902). In 1900, the British issued notes like this. After losing Pretoria and their mint, the Boers retreated and issued gold coins from a blacksmith's shop.

Mount inscribed "Nov 9 1914 HMAS SYDNEY and SMS EMDEN"

War booty

This Mexican silver dollar was part of the booty captured from a German ship by an Australian crew in 1914.

Keepsake

A British soldier made this coin ("From Fred to Nellie") for his wife when he left for World War I.

Revolutionary note

A large issue of notes, like this one (above) for 10 pesos, was made in 1900 by the treasury at the province of Ocana in Colombia, South America, to pay soldiers in the army of General Urribe.

Smoke or spend?

At the end of World War II, a shortage of coins and notes in Europe meant other desirable objects were used as money. Cigarettes, food, and clothing, all in short supply, became acceptable means of payment.

Desert rat money

Allied troops serving in Libya in World War II were paid in Italian lire notes (right), the currency of this former Italian colony.

Greek army money

Italian lire were also used in Greece by the occupying Italian army. This note (left), issued in 1944, features Roman twins Romulus and Remus and the wolf that suckled them, as well as pictures of two coins from ancient Rhodes.

The power of money

It is said that the love of money is the root of all evil, and it can be for some – misers love their money, and thieves love other people's! Money has led many people to crime, but it is also linked to luck. Since ancient times, coins have been used to deter demons, bring a safe journey after death, cure the plague, and promise everlasting love.

The Phoenician god Melqart appears on the front of these silver shekels

King Midas

Legendary King Midas (above) was so greedy he asked the gods to let all he touched turn into gold. But his pleasure turned to pain as food, drink, and, finally, his favourite daughter all turned to gold.

The root of all evil

Murder, robbery, arson, and bribery – where there is crime, there is often money. Money itself is a necessary part of everyday life, so why does it often appear as the motive for crime? Are greed and envy, or poverty and need the causes, or do criminals see in money a route to good fortune?

Coin clippings

Before coin-making machines, coins were not perfectly round. It was easy to trim a bit off silver coins for melting down, so the coins could still be spent. These coils (top left) were clipped from silver English coins in the 17th century.

Beware... pirates!

Spanish treasure fleets shipping silver pieces of eight and gold doubloons from Mexico to Europe were the target of pirates who buried treasure for their retirement.

These coins were issued by Chinese Emperor Kangxi (1661–1722), and the characters of his name, meaning health and prosperity, are on the coins

Keepsake for a child who died aged 18 months

Hearts and doves symbolizing love

Tokens of love

In Britain and America, it was the custom for engaged couples to exchange coins as pledges of love (right). Tokens were also made as keepsakes of dead loved ones or exiled convicts, or to commemorate a new birth.

MARY RAMSHAW BORN MAY 4 –1773– s AGED 18 MONTH DIED OCT 10 1774

Will Culling BORN April 16th 1790

Thirty pieces of silver

The betrayal of Jesus by his follower, Judas, had its cash reward: 30 silver pieces. The coins were probably silver shekels from the Phoenician city of Tyre. These were the only silver coins available in bulk in 1st-century Palestine.

Are you a miser?

Looking after your money is no bad thing, but if you become so mean that you do not spend any of it, then you have become a victim of the power of money.

Demon-dispelling sword for driving off a fever demon

Red is a lucky colour for the Chinese

Corpse hands over his fare to Charon the ferryman

Healing sword and coins

This Chinese coin sword was meant to ward off evil spirits. British monarchs gave sick subjects gold coins to cure them. In Germany, silver medals prevented the plague.

Money, myth, and magic

Money is seen as a source of good fortune. Rich people can afford to buy all of the material goods they need to be happy. But there is a more magical and spiritual side to money. The pictures and words on coins add to their "power" to bring good luck.

"Any fares please?"

According to mythology, the ancient Greeks put a silver coin, "obol", into the mouth of a corpse to pay Charon the ferryman to take the corpse across the Styx River into Hades (above).

This note claims to be an issue of the Bank of Hell

Holy coins

Travellers wore a silver coin charm to win the protection of St George, patron saint of horsemen (above). Indian Muslims carried the name of Mohammed on a silver rupee.

Hell money

The Chinese send money to their dead ancestors by burning special bank notes.

The monkey god, Hanuman, guardian of those in need

Millionaire's club

Gold coin of Roman Emperor Diocletian (284–305 CE)

Queen Anne gold coin (1703) made from captured Spanish treasure

Prize stamp
A Penny Black stamp costs between £160 ($240) and £3,000 ($4,500), depending on its condition.

If you suddenly became a member of the millionaires club, what would you do with your newly acquired wealth? Would you rush out and spend it all at once, or plan carefully and make investments? Or would you save it all, never spending or giving any away? It is harder than you think to spend millions. Like many young millionaires, you could buy designer clothes, computer games, mobile phones, and holidays, but you would still have a lot left.

Ancient Greek silver coin (c. 460 BCE)

Rare coins
These three coins (actual size, above) are each worth thousands of pounds. The Roman coin, the English five-guinea coin of Queen Anne, and the ancient Greek 10-drachma coin have value because they are rare. But you do not need to be a millionaire to collect coins.

Stacks of money
Here are 10,000 one-hundred US dollar bills – a total of $1 million (£665,000). Microsoft co-founder Bill Gates is the world's richest man, with $79.3 billion (£52.7 billion) in 2015.

Modern gambling chips

Display board showing latest bid in five currencies

Going, going, gone!

People can spend a lot of money in an auction room – often much more than they intended to. The bid for the painting in this picture has reached $97,260 (£64,630) – almost one-tenth of the stack of dollars on this page.

Monte Carlo madness

Some people enjoy gambling with their money. For them, the excitement of playing games of chance to increase their fortune is often an addiction. Even if they lose, they still dream of winning a fortune. Monte Carlo in Monaco is a famous gambling centre for the rich. This gambling chip from the 1930s is worth one million French francs.

SOCIÉTÉ DES BAINS DE MER
1.000.000
MONACO

A fortune can be won or lost in the roll of a dice

If you're smart or lucky at cards, your fortune may grow. But if you're not smart, or are unlucky, it may disappear!

Fine wine?

Buying old wine is a gamble not many people are willing to try. The wine of Château Lafite is famous, and a bottle of 1902 vintage costs about £460 ($700) at auction. However, there is a high risk that wine of such a great age is undrinkable, so most collectors leave the bottle unopened and just enjoy looking at it!

MIS EN BOUTEILLES AU CHÂTEAU

CHATEAU LAFITE-ROTHSCHILD
1902

APPELLATION PAUILLAC CONTROLÉE

Shared currencies

The euro symbol
A new symbol was created for the new euro in 1999.

When two or more governments share a common currency, it is called a monetary union. The earliest monetary unions date back to ancient Greece, while in 1999 the euro was introduced in many European countries. Some forms of currency prove popular, such as the everyday use of the US dollar in many parts of the world.

Byzantine   **Ummayad**

Rivals united
The Christian Byzantine Empire and its rival, the Muslim Ummayad Caliphate, used the same coin, based on the solidus of the former Roman Empire. The Byzantine coin features Christ; the Ummayad coin has the declaration of the Islamic faith.

Latin Monetary Union

A forerunner of the European Economic and Monetary Union, the Latin Monetary Union was established by France with Belgium, Italy, Switzerland, and Greece, in 1865. Members kept their own currency name and coin and note designs, but they all used a common unit of currency.

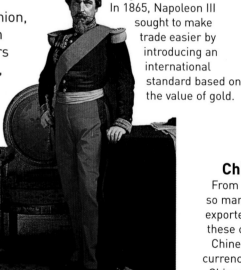

Napoleon III
In 1865, Napoleon III sought to make trade easier by introducing an international standard based on the value of gold.

Portrait of Napoleon III

Swiss franc   **Belgian franc**   **French franc**

Italian lira   **Greek drachma**

Gold and silver
The gold and silver coins of the Latin Union members matched in size and weight, but each country used its own denomination system.

Chinese cash

Javanese cash

Chinese exports
From the tenth century CE, so many Chinese coins were exported to the Far East that these countries adopted the Chinese coins as standard currency. By the 15th century, Chinese coins were used in Java, India, and East Africa.

African Union

In Africa, the trading activities of European imperial powers led to foreign currencies. Some powers established a common monetary system in all of the countries they ruled.

French Africa
France set up two monetary unions based on the franc in its central and western territories.

German rupee   **Italian rupee**

Common coins
British, German, Portuguese, and Italian colonies in East Africa issued coins based on the silver rupee.

25-franc note West African States

100-franc note, Central African States

European Union

The euro was introduced in 1999 into 11 European Union (EU) states. This marked the start of the European Economic and Monetary Union, formed to strengthen economic power and unity. Bank notes and coins denominated in euros and cents were made to replace the national currencies. By 2015, 19 countries were using the euro.

European side
Each euro coin has a European design on one side for all member states, and national designs on the other.

Ireland   Austria   Spain

Finland   Italy   Portugal

Germany   Netherlands   France

Belgium

National side
These coins show the national designs of the first euro countries.

European Union
Conceived in 1957, the EU consists of European countries working together. Nineteen members were part of the Economic and Monetary Union in 2015.

Denomination
The euro has notes ranging from 500 euros down to 5 euros, and coins from 2 euros down to 1 cent. There are eight bank notes and seven coins.

200-euro note

Initials of the European Central Bank

100-euro note

Symbols
The map of Europe and the circle of stars on the EU flag serve as symbols of the Economic and Monetary Union on euro coins and notes.

For security reasons, only specimen notes and coins are shown

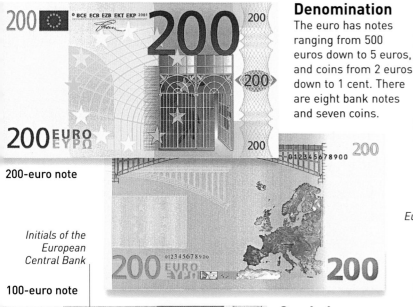

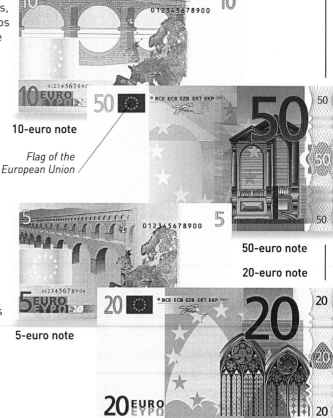

10-euro note

Flag of the European Union

50-euro note

20-euro note

5-euro note

Windows, gateways, and bridges
The fronts of euro notes carry designs representing windows and gateways, while bridges are depicted on their backs. These represent Europe's architectural heritage.

France

Before France adopted the euro in 1999, the currency was francs. The oldest known French money is Greek silver coins made in Massilia (Marseilles), 2,500 years ago. From the 2nd century BCE, the Gauls (Celtic peoples of ancient France) issued coins that copied Greek designs, but when the Romans conquered, they brought their own coins. German Frankish kings overthrew the Romans and issued silver deniers, the first true French coins. The franc became the main unit of French currency in 1795.

The Greek goddess Artemis

Greek silver coins
In the 5th century BCE, the Greek colony at Massilia issued small silver coins with various designs, like this one with a ram's head. The colony was rich, and from 350 BCE, its silver coins were widely used by Celtic peoples.

Patron saint of coin makers
St Eligius, patron saint of coin makers and goldsmiths, worked at the Paris mint during the 7th century for the Merovingian kings of Gaul. In this stained-glass panel he is shown using traditional tools for making coins.

Celtic gold
The Greek god Apollo on this gold coin (100 BCE) was copied by the Celts from an earlier Greek coin.

Back

Front

Warrior
On this silver coin of the Roman Republic, a Gaulish chief is on the front and his war chariot is on the back. The coin was made in 48 BCE, after Julius Caesar conquered Gaul.

Prow of Roman galley

Roman Gaul coin
The letters "CIV" on this coin stand for "Colonia Julia Viennensis", which means the "Colony of Julius Caesar at Vienne". Vienne is in the south of France; this coin was made there in about 36 BCE.

Louis XIV chose the sun as his emblem because he saw himself as the powerful centre of the Universe

"Le Bel"
Philippe IV, who reigned from 1285–1314, was known as "le Bel" (the Fair). Until the time of Philippe, gold coins were scarce.

"LUD" is the abbreviation of "Ludivicus", the Latin form of "Louis"

Silver sun king
From Francis I (1515–1547), portraits of French kings featured on coins. King Louis XIV (the "Sun King") is on this écu. The European Economic Community revived the name ECU (European Currency Unit) for its new common currency unit.

Silver denier and gros
Charlemagne (742–814) issued this denier (left). It was the only denomination used in France until the silver gros (right) was brought by King Louis IX, in 1266.

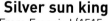

The denomination "sol" was popularly known as "sou"

Paper money

From 1790 until 1793, the French Revolution was funded by issues of paper money known as "assignats". Coins were still issued using the pre-revolutionary denominations.

5-livre coin of Louis XVI issued in 1792, the year before he was executed on the guillotine

Royal portrait is replaced by Hercules, Liberty, and Equality on this 5-franc coin of 1795

First Republic, 1792–1804

Second Republic, 1848–1852

Napoleon Bonaparte appeared on coins from 1802 when he was Consul of the Republic.

Third Republic, 1871–1940

Money to burn

As too many "assignats" were issued, notes became worthless. In 1796, these notes were burned.

Five Mariannes

From 1793, the main design of French Republican coinage was a female head to represent the Republic. The image was known as "Marianne". These five versions are the coins of the five Republics.

Distinctive raised mark for recognition by those with impaired sight

Metallic ink security feature

Fifth Republic, 1958–present day

Fourth Republic, 1945–1958

Local money

In World War I, small change was issued locally. Coins and notes, like this Grenoble note, were issued by local trade associations.

Special coins

Commemorative coins are issued for general circulation. This franc celebrates the 30th anniversary of Charles de Gaulle as President.

Today's money

Since 1 January 1999, the euro has been the official currency of France, replacing the French franc.

FF20　FF10

FF5　FF2　FF1

20c　10c　5c

Germany

Until the introduction of the euro on 1 January 1999, the mark was the currency of Germany, although in different forms when the country was divided between 1945 and 1990. The mark, divided into 100 pfennigs, was introduced in 1871 when Wilhelm I, King of Prussia, formed the German empire. Before the empire was established, the German kingdoms, states, and cities each had their own currency system.

This engraving shows a Mint Master weighing out coins in the 14th century

Conrad II, King of Saxony (1024–1039)

Roman gold
This large gold coin was made at the mint in Trier to reward soldiers serving the Roman Emperor Constantius I (293–306 BCE).

Coin issued in Rhenish Palatine showing St John the Baptist

Coin issued in Trier showing St Peter

Silver pfennigs
Early pfennigs used French and English designs, but in the 12th century, many German designs appeared on broader, thinner versions. The coin above left was issued by Emperor Frederick I Barbarossa (1152–1190), and the coin above right by Otto I of Brandenburg (1157–1184).

In this 15th-century Swiss drawing, coin makers are minting small silver pfennigs

Coin issued in Basel showing the Virgin Mary

Gold gulden
Gold coins began to be issued in quantity during the 14th century. They were the same size as Italian florins.

Thaler of Count Stephen of Slick, 1519

Thaler of Johan Wilhelm, Duke of Saxony, 1569

The arm of God crowns the horse

Silver thalers
In the 15th century, the discovery of silver mines in Joachimsthal in Bohemia (present-day Austria) led to new, large, silver coins, called Joachimsthalers, or "thalers". Silver from the mines was exported throughout Western Europe.

The horse leaping over the silver mines is the symbol of Luneburg

4-thaler coin of Christian Ludwig, Duke of Brunswick-Luneburg, 1662

Frederick the Great of Prussia
Frederick, the Philosopher King (1740–1786), reorganized his coinage system so it was based on the thaler and the pfennig. This gold coin (above), struck at Berlin in 1750, was worth 10 thalers.

Prince and Pope

A revival of Roman Empire coin designs appeared in Italy in the late 15th century, with life-like portraits of rulers. The ruler on the silver coin (above left) is Cosimo Medici of Florence (1536–1574), and the gold coin (below left) shows Pope Leo X (1513–1521) of the wealthy Medici family.

Austrian coin

Sardinian coin

Spanish coin

Contending powers

A copper coin of Austrian Empress Maria Theresa (1740–1780), a gold coin of Vittorio Amadeo of Savoy, King of Sardinia (1773–1796), and a silver coin of Ferdinand IV, Spanish king of the Two Sicilies (1759–1825), represent the three powers fighting for control of Italy.

Roman "assignat"

In 1798, the Pope-ruled states rejected his authority and together formed the Roman Republic, issuing their own "assignats" (right).

Year 7 of the French Republic

Lire note

The lira became Italy's national currency in 1861, when Vittorio Emanuele II became King of Italy.

Italian bankers

The practice of banking first began in the 14th century in northern Italy, in the area known as Lombardy. This was the start of modern commercial banking.

Bimetallic coin

New money

Since 1 January 1999, the euro has been the official currency of Italy, replacing the lira.

Signatures of bank officials

Political coin

This 1923, 2-lire coin of King Vittorio Emanuele III used the Fascist emblem (sticks and an axe). In protest, a coin user stamped on the Communist emblem (hammer and sickle).

Small change

A lack of small coins in the 1970s forced shopkeepers to give telephone tokens and sweets as change.

Spain and Portugal

In 1492, Christopher Columbus set out from Spain to open up a westward route to the East, and found the Americas. Six years later, Vasco da Gama from Portugal opened the sea route around Africa to India. These two events dramatically changed the history of money. They led to the issue of new European-style coins in the Americas, Africa, and, eventually, Asia, and also brought to Europe vast amounts of gold and silver from those continents.

Spanish and Portuguese galleons were often loaded with treasure

Carthaginian coin, Spain, 210 BCE

Greek coin from Emporium, 250 BCE

Spanish Celtic coin, c. 100 BCE

Coin of Carthaginian settlement at Salacia in Portugal, c. 100 BCE

Ancient coins
Greek colonists had introduced coinage into Spain and Portugal by the 4th century BCE. Their main mint was at Emporium (now Ampurias) in northeast Spain.

Spanish Roman copper coin from Saragossa, c. 20 CE

Visigoth gold coin

Moorish gold coin

Coin from Castile, copying a Moorish design

Portuguese gold coin

Moorish gold
In 711, an Arab-led Moorish army conquered the Visigoths in Spain and issued their own coins. The Islamic designs on Moorish coins were copied on the earliest coins of the Christian kings of Castile and Portugal by the 15th century.

Roman aqueduct of Segovia, the mark of the Segovian mint

New worlds
The search for spices and gold took Columbus to the Americas, and Vasco da Gama to India. The gold they found was used to make coins such as these.

Silver "pieces of eight"

Robinson Crusoe

Gold doubloon

Spanish empire
The Spanish conquerors of the Americas exploited the rich gold sources and silver mines in Mexico, Bolivia, and Peru. Silver pieces of eight and gold doubloons were loaded on treasure ships to Europe.

"I got all my cargo on shore... I found there were three great bags of pieces of eight... and wrapped up in paper, six doubloons of gold."

Portuguese empire
Portugal's empire in the Indian Ocean was based on trade. This tin coin of 1511 was used at Malacca port in Malaya. In 1693, gold found in Brazil was made into coins like this Portuguese example.

Conquistadors
Spanish conquistadors fought the Inca and Aztec peoples of the Americas for their gold and silver.

50-reales coin of Spanish American silver

Original VIII (eight) stamp

Money troubles
The flow of silver and gold into Spain made it the world's richest country, but it wasted money on war. Prices went up and copper coins were revalued.

XII (twelve) stamp revaluing coin

Joseph Napoleon

Ferdinand VII

Duke of Wellington

Spanish kings
In 1808 two new kings were crowned in Spain: the legitimate heir, Ferdinand VII, and Napoleon's brother, Joseph. A British army drove the French usurper out. Both kings issued their own coins.

Portuguese war note
After the Napoleonic War, civil war continued in Portugal. This 1805 note was reissued in 1828 by the usurper, Miguel I.

Lisboa 1805 N.° R.¹ 1$200

Civil war
The Spanish Republican government issued this note in the Civil War (1936–1939). Later, coins featured General Franco, the victorious anti-republican.

"Liberty and democracy"
These words are inscribed on this Portuguese coin to celebrate the restoration of democratic government in 1974.

Spain

			5000

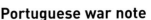

Pta 50   Pta 100   Pta 25   Pta 5

Ferdinand and Isabella were patrons of Christopher Columbus

Portugal

Esc 200   Esc 100   Esc 50   Esc 20

Today's money
On 1 January 1999, the euro replaced the peseta in Spain and the escudo in Portugal.

Greece and Turkey

"As rich as Croesus"
This saying refers to the wealth of Croesus, King of Lydia (c. 560–547 BCE), who issued one of the first gold coins.

Today's coins all have their origin in the ancient Greek versions of the coins first made in ancient Turkey. The ancient Greeks gave coins their round shape with designs on both sides. Since then, Greece and Turkey have had many rulers – Greek, Persian, Roman, Byzantine, Turkish, French, Italian, British, Russian, and German – who have all issued coins of their own. The Greek drachma and the Turkish lira are of quite recent origin.

Royal images
Greek kings can be seen on these two silver coins; Philip II of Macedonia (359–336 BCE) on horseback, and Antiochus I of Syria (281–261 BCE).

Greek writing was used in the Byzantine Empire

Byzantine gold
The Byzantine Emperor Alexius II (1297–1330), issued coins like this in Constantinople (now Istanbul), Turkey, and Thessalonika, Greece.

Flying pig
This coin's design and inscription identify it as a 5th-century-BCE issue of the city of Lalysus, on the Greek island of Rhodes.

Coin issued for Mark Antony before the battle of Actium (31 BCE)

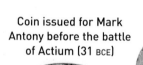

Romans
The Romans issued coins in what is now Greece and Turkey. The gold coin is a Greek issue for Mark Antony. The bronze coin from Turkey features Roman Emperor Caracalla.

Suleiman the magnificent
Suleiman, the most powerful Ottoman sultan (1494–1566), issued the gold coin below. His reign was noted for its military power.

Seated warrior is holding a severed head

Lion's face coin

The Crusades
The silver coin (top) was issued by a French crusader. The copper coins were made by forces fighting for eastern Turkey. The lion's face coin (above left) was issued by the Christian Armenian kings of Cilicia (1187–1218), and the warrior coin (left) by the Turkish rulers of Mardin.

Silver aqche of Thessalonika (Salonika), 1574

Gold altin of Istanbul, 1520

Sultan's money
The Turkish Ottoman sultans ruled Greece and Turkey. They issued their pictureless coins throughout their vast empire. The knotted emblem (known as a *tughra*) on the silver coin and the note is the official "signature" of the sultans.

Tughra emblem

Paper kurus of the Ottoman Imperial Bank, 1877

Silver kurus of Istanbul, 1769

The phoenix, symbol of rebirth, taken from a Greek banknote

Venetian copper soldo of the 18th century

Coins of Corfu

For a long time, Corfu and the other Ionian islands were the only parts of Greece to escape Turkish Ottoman rule. From 1402 until 1797 they were ruled by Venice. They became part of Greece in 1863.

Russian copper gazetta, 1801

British copper obol, 1819

Otto I gold coin

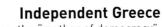

Independent Greece

In 1828, Greece, the "mother of democracy", achieved independence from Turkish rule. In 1831, Greece became a kingdom under Otto I of Bavaria, who features on the 20-drachma coin.

Greek Republic copper coin

Corfu cricket

During the British occupation of Corfu, the British troops missed their game of cricket, so they built a cricket field in Corfu town. The game is still played there by the Greeks.

National Bank of Greece one-drachma note, 1885

Island money

The Greek island of Thasos remained under Turkish rule until 1914. This Turkish copper coin was countermarked by Greeks in Thasos in 1893.

Old designs

The Second Greek Republic (1925–1935) used ancient Greek coin designs on new issues. This one features Athena, from an ancient Corinth coin.

Today's money: Turkey

The Turkish lira (pound) is divided into 100 kurus (piastre), but kurus coins are not issued.

Turkey

TL 50,000

TL 25,000

TL 10,000

Turkish republic

In 1923, Ottoman rule in Turkey ceased, and it became a republic under the leadership of Kamel Ataturk, seen on this 1934 coin.

Greece

Local Greek note

In World War II, many locally issued notes were in use. This 5,000-drachma note is from Zagora.

Today's money: Greece

Since 2001, the euro has been Greece's currency, replacing the drachma.

Coin of King Cnut (1019–1035) from his mint at Lund

Norwegian penny of Viking King Olaf Kyrre (1067–1093)

Silver pennies
English designs were copied on early Danish and Norwegian pennies.

Denmark and Norway

Before Denmark and Norway had their own coins, the Vikings introduced French, German, English, and Islamic coins they had captured as loot or acquired in trade. In the 10th and 11th centuries, the Danish and Norwegian kings issued their own coins, with designs copied from English silver pennies. Today, Denmark and Norway both use the krone, divided into 100 øre, as their currency. The same denominations are used in Sweden. These three currencies were introduced in 1873 as part of a common Scandinavian system.

Cnut rules the waves
Legendary King Cnut of Denmark and England tried to prove his power by stopping the tide, but failed. He issued English-style pennies in both kingdoms.

King of two kingdoms
King Christian IV (1588–1648) was king of both Denmark and Norway, but he issued separate coins for each kingdom. The silver coin on the left is Danish, and the one on the right is Norwegian.

The letter "C" is the initial of the king who issued this klippe, Christian V

Royal gifts
Square coins, called klippe, were issued in Denmark during the 16th and 17th centuries. They were emergency issues in war because they were quick to make. These two klippe were made for the king.

Pillars and globe design copied from a "piece of eight"

The Lapp reindeer herders of northern Norway used reindeer and furs as payments

Trade coins
This silver coin (left) was made in 1777 for the Danish Asiatic Society to use in China. The gold coin (1726) shows Christiansborg, a Danish settlement in West Africa where the gold used to make the coin came from.

Money marks
In the 18th century, the monetary system in Denmark and Norway was based on the mark, which divided into 16 skillings. This krone of 1723 (right) was worth 4 marks; 64 of the copper skillings (far right) made a krone.

A Viking warship

The lion-with-axe design was used on Norwegian coins. There are four on these pages.

Dalers

In 1813, Denmark issued a currency based on a daler of 96 skillings. The daler was still used after it came under control of the King of Sweden in 1814. These are examples of daler notes and silver dalers.

Nō. 51721a

E e n Rigs-   bankdaler.

Saa Anfordring indloser Rigsbanken i Kiobenhavn denne Anviisning med I. Rbdlr., og validerer den imidlertid som Rigsbankpenge efter Fundationen af 5 Januar dens 4 §.
Udstædt efter Rigsbankens Fuldmagt og paa dens Vegne.
Christiania den 6 Jan: 1814

Not.

Danish coins

Dolphin and grain symbolize fishing and agriculture

Norwegian coins

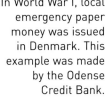

Paper krone

In World War I, local emergency paper money was issued in Denmark. This example was made by the Odense Credit Bank.

Scandinavian money

In 1873, a unified currency system was created for Denmark, Norway, and Sweden. The same denominations were issued by each country, but with different designs.

Emergency coins

In World War II, there was a copper shortage because copper was used to make shell cases. Instead of copper, Norway issued iron coins (above left), while Denmark made coins of aluminum (above right) and zinc.

Norway

NKr 10   NKr 1   50 øre

Today's money

Denmark and Norway use the same currency names. The krone was adopted by both countries in 1873.

Denmark

DKr 1

25 øre

1 øre

Sweden and Finland

As well as issuing Europe's first paper money, Sweden issued the biggest coins ever – copper plate money. Coins could weigh 19 kg (42 lb). Today, Sweden's money is based on the krona, divided into 100 öre. Finland used Swedish money until 1809, when the country came under Russian control and currency.

Swedish copies
The coin (above left) copies an Islamic coin. English visitors made the penny

One-sided coins
Silver pennies with a design on one side only were made in the 13th century. The M is for Sweden's King Magnus.

Dalers, ducats, and öre
In 1534, Gustav I (1523–1560) introduced Sweden's first silver daler (above left). Gustav II (1611–1632) introduced Sweden's first copper coinage, square pieces denominated in öre (above right). Swedish rule extended into Germany, and Gustav II issued gold ducats for his subjects there.

Man-powered drop hammers stamped designs onto plate money

Plate money
Sweden first issued huge copper coins called plate money during Kristina's reign. Plate money was very heavy; this square one daler (right) weighs almost 2 kg (4 lb), so paper money, like the cheque for 288 dalers (above), was used instead.

Daler tokens

In 1717 the Swedish government ran out of money. It issued paper and small copper dalers instead of plate money. The copper dalers were decorated with pictures of Roman gods.

Copper dalers

Paper daler

Notes were only valid if all three signatures appeared

Russian Imperial two-headed eagle

This design is taken from a Finnish bank note; the name of the Bank of Finland is written in Swedish, Finnish, and Russian.

Russian Finland

In 1809, Sweden lost control of Finland to Russia. The Russians introduced roubles and kopeks. Finland was given its own currency in 1864, with coins denominated in markkaa, divided into 100 penniä.

Common coins

Sweden's money has been denominated in krona and öre since 1873 when, along with Denmark and Norway, it reorganized its currency to form a common system.

Gold 20 krona

5-öre coin

Independence

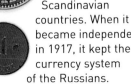

Finland had a different coinage system from the other Scandinavian countries. When it became independent in 1917, it kept the currency system of the Russians.

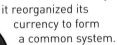
Fmk 10

Fmk 2

Fmk 1

Finland

Sweden

SKr 5　**SKr 1**　**50 öre**

Today

Since 1 January 1999, the euro has been Finland's currency. Sweden's currency is based on the krona.

United Kingdom

All the regions of the United Kingdom of Great Britain and Northern Ireland now use a monetary system based on the pound sterling (£) divided into 100 pennies. Different forms of paper money circulate in each region, except England and Wales, which share Bank of England notes. Celts and Romans introduced coins into Britain, and Britain has since been responsible for introducing its own money to many parts of the world, largely through trade and conquest.

The Royal Mint was located in or near the Tower of London for almost 1,000 years

Celtic gold

This Celtic coin from c. 10–40 CE names an ancient British king, Cunobelin, King of the Catuvellauni tribe

Roman mint
The Roman mint in London made this bronze coin for Emperor Maximian.

Saxon and Viking pennies
The Anglo-Saxons introduced the silver penny (above). The coin on the left shows Alfred the Great, and the right names Viking Eric Bloodaxe.

Silver sixpence

Machine-made money
In 1566, the silver sixpence of Elizabeth was the first to be made with a screw-press coining machine like in the Royal mint picture (above).

Scottish kings always faced to the side on sterling pennies

Sterling silver
King Edward I introduced a new silver penny, the sterling, in 1279. His coins were so often used in trade that many foreign copies were made. These coins are sterlings of Edward I (left) and Robert Bruce, King of Scotland.

Punch marks to test the coin was solid gold

Groat and noble
As trade expanded in the 14th century, the silver penny was joined by more valuable coins. This silver groat was worth four pennies, and the gold noble 80 pennies.

18th-century small change
Local small change reappeared in the late 18th century when the government failed to issue copper coins. Local traders issued their own copper tokens.

The Queen's Head public house, London

Welsh druid halfpenny

Small change
In the 17th century, a shortage of small change prompted traders to issue brass farthings (quarter penny) and halfpennies.

Copper halfpenny
Britain's first copper halfpenny of 1672 featured Britannia on the coin's back.

Lady Godiva coin

Lady Godiva
According to legend, Lady Godiva rode naked through Coventry to get her husband to lower the heavy taxes.

Thick-rimmed 1797 steam-press coins were called cartwheels.

Gold sovereign

King Henry VII issued the first British pound coin (worth 240 silver pennies) in 1489. This one (c. 1545) was made for King Henry VIII.

Gold unite

King James I issued a new pound coin in 1604. This one was made in the English Civil War, when Parliament ruled England after James' son, Charles I, was executed.

Gold pound

This machine-made, gold pound (1663) depicts King Charles II.

Gold sovereign

Called a sovereign, a new pound coin was issued in King George III's reign (1738–1820).

Queen Victoria liked to give 5-pound coins like this one as a souvenir to her court visitors

Decimal coins

In 1849, an attempt at decimalization (division into units of 10) brought a new 2-shilling coin, the florin (one-tenth of a pound). This was a 10-pence coin after full decimalization in 1971.

The 1849 florin

1971 equivalent 10-pence coin

Paper guinea

Paper money became popular in Britain during the 18th century. This Scottish guinea note of 1777 was the first to be printed in three colours.

£2	£1	50p	20p
10p	5p	2p	1p

Today

The UK has a national currency based on the pound sterling, divided into 100 pennies.

£1 Jersey	5p Isle of Man	2p Guernsey

Scotland

Northern Ireland

Wartime sixpence note

The Island of Jersey issued locally designed notes during World War II.

The United States

American bald eagle

The currency of the United States of America is dollars and cents. Coins and paper money were first introduced to North America by European settlers. The dollar had already been chosen as the currency before the Declaration of Independence was signed on 4 July 1776. The first US dollars were paper, with silver dollars also issued from 1794. Today's paper US dollar is the world's most widely used currency.

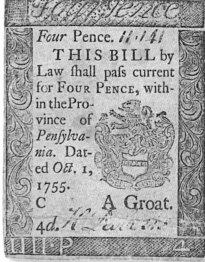

British colonial money
British colonists did not have British coins, so they used beads and tobacco, and made coins and paper money. This was in pounds, shillings, and pence like these Massachusetts shillings of 1652 and Pennsylvanian 4-pence note of 1755.

First coins of the United States
The United States issued a regular coinage based on the dollar in 1793. The 1793 copper cent (top right) was followed by the silver dollar in 1794 (top centre), and gold 10-dollar "eagle" in 1795 (top left).

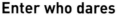

Chain on this tin pattern represents the 13 states united against Britain

Continental currency
When the colonists broke with Britain, they financed their Revolutionary War with paper dollars issued by the Continental Congress.

Leaf money
Bundles of tobacco leaves were official money in Virginia and Maryland in the 17th and 18th centuries.

Enter who dares
Fort Knox in Kentucky has been the site of the United States Gold Bullion Depository since 1938. Gold is stored in concrete and steel vaults inside a heavily guarded bomb-proof building.

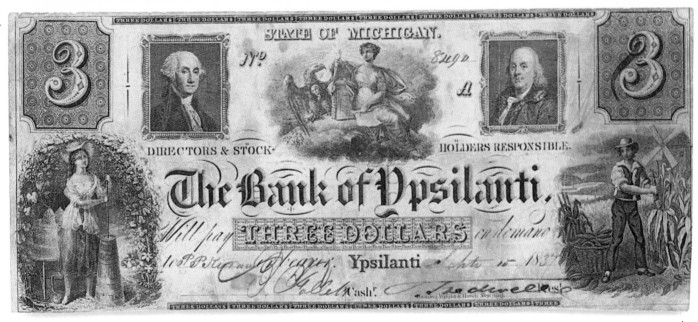

Three-dollar bill
During the 19th century, most of the money used in the United States was in the form of paper dollars. This note was issued in 1837 by a small private bank in Ypsilanti, Michigan.

Gold rush
After the discovery of gold in California in 1848, gold dust and nuggets were used as money in mining camps. In San Francisco gold was made into coins like this 50-dollar piece from 1852.

Depression breadline
After the Wall Street Crash of 1929, the value of the dollar fell drastically. By the end of 1931, 4,000 banks had closed. There was massive unemployment, and many people had to rely on charity to eat, lining up for regular food hand-outs.

Seal of the Department of the Treasury

Eisenhower dollar
Recent coins have a presidential portrait: Eisenhower on the dollar (right); Kennedy on the half-dollar; Washington on the quarter; Franklin D Roosevelt on the dime; Jefferson on the nickel; and Lincoln on the cent.

Time to celebrate
Commemorative coins were issued on the 200th anniversary of American Independence in 1976.

Failed dollar
In 1979, a dollar coin portraying feminist leader Susan B Anthony was issued. It was not popular, and was withdrawn from use.

Las Vegas
Dollar coins survive in the casinos of Las Vegas and Atlantic City, New Jersey, where they are used in slot machines.

25 cents "quarter"   **10 cents** "dime"   **5 cents** "nickel"   **1 cent** "penny"

Today's money
US currency is based on the dollar, divided into 100 cents.

Canada

British and French settlers introduced coins and bank notes to Canada, but the native peoples continued to use traditional payment, such as beads and blankets. The dollar-and-cent currency of today was issued in the 1850s. The Dominion of Canada, established in 1867, adopted the dollar as its official currency in 1868.

Canadian coin
Canada's first coins were made in Paris for French settlers on the orders of Louis XIV of France.

Beaver money
The Hudson Bay (Trading) Company issued paper money and brass tokens, but traders used beaver skins as money.

Nova Scotia penny token, 1824

Upper Canada halfpenny token, 1833

Provincial tokens
British sterling was the official money of Canada until the 1850s, but most provinces had currencies based on Spanish and American dollars. Local tokens were made for small change. In English-speaking provinces, they were pennies and halfpennies. In French-speaking Quebec, tokens were in sou.

Lower Canada sou token, 1837

Lower Canada 2-sou token, 1837

British Columbian gold

In 1862, this 20-dollar coin was made in British Columbia from local gold.

The native Indians traded furs for more exotic goods with British and French settlers.

Provincial coins

From 1858, when the Province of Canada (Ontario and Quebec) introduced a bronze cent, similar coins were introduced in other provinces. The first coin is from Prince Edward Island (1871), the second from Nova Scotia (1861), and the third from Newfoundland (1938).

Ten Canadian dollars

This 1906 note of the Montreal office of the Merchants Bank of Canada is denominated in dollars. The Currency Act of 1868 established the dollar as the currency of the Dominion of Canada.

Silver 50-cent coin

Bronze 1-cent coin

Dollar coin

Beaver 5-cent coin

Totem pole design

Dominion coins

The first coins of the Dominion of Canada – silver 50, 25, 10, and 5 cents – were issued in 1870. A bronze cent came in 1876. The first dollar coin was 1935. Recent issues feature wildlife designs.

Royal Canadian "Mountie"

New coins

The Royal Canadian Mint's commemorative coins include these dollars marking the centenaries of British Columbia, and the Royal Canadian Mounted Police.

Plastic chip

This plastic 1-dollar gambling chip is from Diamond Tooth Gertie's casino in Yukon.

$2

$1

25 cents

10 cent

Today's money

Canadian currency is based on the dollar divided into 100 cents.

5 cent

1 cent

Australasia

British pounds, shillings, and pence arrived in Australia and New Zealand with British settlers, but visiting trade ships made Indian, Dutch, Spanish, and Portuguese coins more common. In 1792, Sydney Cove settlers found new money when an American ship delivered a cargo of rum. This liquid was money in New South Wales until it was replaced in 1813 by Spanish American silver dollars. Australia introduced today's dollar currencies in 1966, and New Zealand in 1967.

Gold!
In 1851, gold was found in Australia. Gold dust was used as money until 1852, when ingots (above) and unofficial "Kangaroo Office" coins were made. In 1853, a new mint in Sydney made sovereigns (right).

"Holey dollar" and "dump"
From 1813 until 1822, dollars with a hole were the currency of New South Wales. The silver "dump" cut from the middle was also official money.

The great gold rush
The discovery of gold in Australia prompted many to search for it.

Tokens and notes
Although British coins were the official currency of New Zealand, most money in use during the 19th century was locally issued copper tokens, and notes like this, issued in 1857 by a British bank. More than 140 different tokens like those above were also issued.

Thames Goldfields penny token, 1874

"Advance New Zealand" penny token, 1881

BANK OF QUEENSLAND, LIMITED.

TOOWOOMBA

THREE | THREE

№ 1725 | № 1725

I Promise to pay the Bearer on Demand, this Sum of **THREE POUNDS** in Cash here. Brisbane 2nd Jan 1865.

Batho & Co London.

FOR THE BANK OF QUEENSLAND, LIMITED.

THREE

Ent. *William Anderson* ACCt. | *A Anderson* MANAGER.

BRISBANE.

Australia's flightless, swift-running bird, the emu

Barter
When Europeans reached Australia and New Zealand, they swapped cloth and tools for food with the Aboriginal and Maori peoples.

Taking note
In the later 19th century, bank notes and local tokens provided most Australian money. The Bank of Queensland issued this three-pound note in 1865. The copper tokens are from Tasmania and Western Australia.

Australian coins
In 1910, the Australians minted their own Commonwealth coins, including shillings, silver florins, sixpences, and bronze pennies.

NZ$2

NZ$1

20 cents

New Zealand

New Zealand coins
In 1933 New Zealand got its own coins, including florins (left) and shillings (bottom left). Bronze pennies (below) were made from 1940.

This Maori "good luck" image (*tiki*) featured on the halfpenny from 1940 to 1965.

A$2

A$1

50 cents

Plastic bank note with transparent window for security

Australia

Today's money
Australia and New Zealand base their currencies on a dollar divided into 100 cents.

China and Japan

The Great Wall of China stretches for 2,400 km (1,500 miles)

The modern currencies of both China and Japan developed from silver dollars introduced by European and American traders, and exchanged for silk, tea, gold, and rhubarb! Dollars (or "round coins") replaced traditional currency. Chinese coinage began in the 6th century BCE, and was later adopted by Japan. Both countries played their part in developing paper money.

A Chinese money changer

Ancient China

Early Chinese coins were made of cast bronze in the shape of tools, like this hoe-shaped coin, c. 300 BCE. In 221 BCE, China's first emperor, Qin Shihuangdi, introduced round coins with square holes.

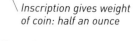

Inscription gives weight of coin: half an ounce

The shogun's coin

In 1626, the shogun of Japan brought new bronze coins. Their inscription meant "generous, ever-lasting money".

Inscription gives the weight (10 ounces) and the mint master's signature

Bamboo money

In 19th-century Shanghai, China, bamboo sticks replaced heavy standard coins as money.

Holes for threading coins on strings

Standard coins

In 621 CE, the Chinese Tang Dynasty introduced a new standard bronze coin (top left) with an inscription around the square hole. This was used in China until 1912. In 708 CE, the same type of coin was introduced into Japan (left).

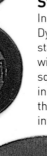

Multiple coin

During a copper shortage in China, "multiple" coins were issued. This one (1854) was worth 1,000 standard coins.

Oban

This oban ("big piece") from 1860 is typical of the gold coins in Japan during the Tokugawa Shogunate (1603–1868).

The figure on this Taiwan dollar is the Chinese god of long life

THE YUE SOO IMPERIAL BANK
KIANGSU PROVINCE

1   1

S. No 135241   S. No 135241

Promises to pay the bearer on demand

ONE SILVER DOLLAR LOCAL CURRENCY

at any of its offices in Kiangsu province for value received

Soochow 1st September, 1906

BY ORDER OF THE GOVERNOR

with the seal of the Treasurer

1   1

Paper dragons
The Chinese also used bank notes valued in dollars.

Chinese dollars
In the 19th century, the Chinese made their own silver dollars (above), including the local Taiwan dollar and the Imperial Dragon dollar.

Meiji emperor
Mutsuhito was Japan's ruler (1868–1912).

"Workers of the world unite"
So reads the slogan on this Chinese dollar (left) issued by the Communist army in 1934.

Japanese dollar
The dollar influenced Japan to adopt this denomination for its own coinage. In 1870, the Meiji emperor replaced the traditional Shogun coins with his own "dragon" dollar (above).

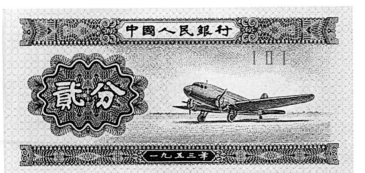

Yuan and fen
The Chinese called their dollar "yuan" (the round coin), and their cent "fen" (meaning a hundredth part).

Yen and sen
The Japanese called their dollar "yen" (the round coin), and their cent "sen" (the name of the traditional bronze coin). This 10-sen note was issued in 1872.

China

yuan   5 jiao   1 jiao

500 yen   10 yen   5 yen   Japan

Today's money
Japan's yen and China's yuan both derive their name from the silver dollars issued in both countries in the 19th century.

Africa

Some of the earliest records of money come from Africa. The first African coins were issued in about 500 BCE by a Greek colony in Libya. Coinage soon became widespread from Egypt to Morocco, as Phoenician, local African, Roman, and Byzantine mints were established. From the 8th century CE onwards, traders took West African gold to the Islamic mints of North Africa, where it was shipped to Europe to make coins. In some areas, traditional currencies, such as cattle, salt, and cloth, have survived to this day.

North

The emblem of Carthage was a horse, shown here as Pegasus

Arabic writing

Carthage
This silver coin paid troops during the wars between Carthage (an ancient Tunisian city) and Rome (264–241) BCE.

Berber gold
The Muwahhid Berber rulers of Morocco took West African gold north across the Sahara Desert.

French Morocco
This 2-franc note was issued in the French Protectorate of Morocco in World War II. French money was used in Morocco from 1910 to 1960.

West

Kissi penny
Until the 1930s, pieces of iron wire were used as money in Liberia and neighbouring West African states. The Kissi people made them.

Portuguese Africa
This copper macuta was issued in Lisbon to use in Angola.

The Nigerian Ibo people used copper rings as money.

BANQUE CENTRALE DES ÉTATS DE L'AFRIQUE DE L'OUEST

100 21871 693121871 G.278

LE PRÉSIDENT, LE DIRECTEUR GÉNÉRAL,

G.278 21871

CENT FRANCS

Lion dollar
The British colony of Sierra Leone became a home for freed African slaves. In 1791 a coinage of silver dollars was made for Sierra Leone.

Liberia
Liberia was also established as a home for freed slaves. Its American founders issued copper cents for the settlement in 1833.

Independence
The Gold Coast was the first British colony to gain independence. It became the nation of Ghana in 1956.

West African monetary union
When the former French West African colonies achieved statehood in 1958, they joined to issue a common currency.

East

Pharaoh's gold

This coin of Pharaoh Nectanebo II (359–343 BCE) has Egyptian hieroglyphs meaning "good gold".

Greek Egypt
Alexander the Great set up Greek rule in Egypt in 332 BCE and features on this coin.

Roman Egypt

After Egyptian Queen Cleopatra died, the Romans ruled Egypt and issued coins, like this copper example.

Thalers in Africa
Before World War II, Ethiopian currency was based on Austrian silver thalers. This note is two thalers in French and Ethiopian.

Swahili coin
The Swahili Sultan of Kilwa in Tanzania issued this coin in the 15th century.

Sudanese ring

This gold ring was used to make payments in Sudan in the 19th century.

French Madagascar: cut fragments of silver 5-franc coin, 1890

Father of the nation

Commemorative coins mark the independence of African states. This one shows Jomo Kenyatta, "Father" of Kenya.

Part of the design from a French Central African bank note

Portuguese Mozambique: gold 2.5 maticaes, 1851

British Mombasa: rupee of the Imperial British East Africa Company (Kenya), 1888

French Madagascar: 10-centimes stamp money, 1916

German East Africa (Tanzania): gold 15 rupees, 1916

South

UN coin
This Zambian 50-ngwee coin was issued in 1969 to promote the work of the United Nations Food and Agriculture Organization.

Coins of South Africa

During apartheid, South African coins had designs of Dutch settlers. Now they show the national arms of South Africa and feature African languages.

5 cents   2 cents

Colonial currencies
France, Germany, Britain, Italy, and Portugal issued coins and notes for their East African colonies. They sometimes matched the issues in use locally, rather than introducing new money. Indian coins were widely used, so in 1888, the British issued a Mombasa rupee for Kenya. Rupees were also issued by the Germans in Tanganyika (now part of Tanzania), and by the Italians in Somalia.

Money matters

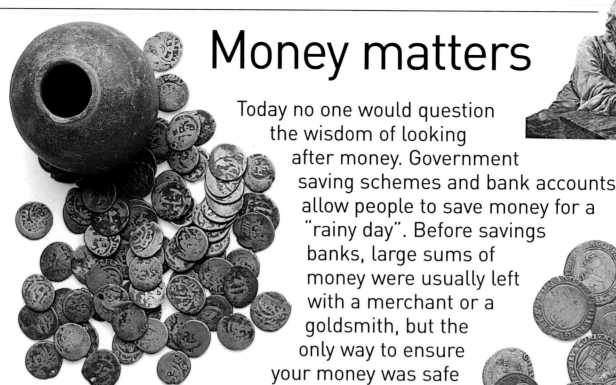

Today no one would question the wisdom of looking after money. Government saving schemes and bank accounts allow people to save money for a "rainy day". Before savings banks, large sums of money were usually left with a merchant or a goldsmith, but the only way to ensure your money was safe was to hide or bury it.

Buried treasure

This hoard of 17th-century Persian silver coins, hidden in a small, blue-glazed pot, was discovered in 1960.

Plastic "purses"

Keeping loose change in your pocket can be a nuisance. Both these gadgets hold British pound coins in place.

Most people these days keep their savings in a bank

The English oak tree emblem appeared on British pound coins during 1987

Leather purse

This purse and the coins it contains were left at a British court in the 18th century. The money was saved for a long time – some coins were 150 years old.

Ring for closing the purse

Opening for coins

Slot for coins

Metal money box

Lose the key to this small metal safe and you will never get your money out! The coins go into a self-sealing slot, and the notes into a curved slot on the other end. Serious savers could leave the key at the bank to avoid the temptation of spending.

Dress purse

This 19th-century dress purse was designed to be worn on a belt, as in this picture. The opening was a slit in the middle that closed by moving the rings to each end, but this was really not pickpocket proof!

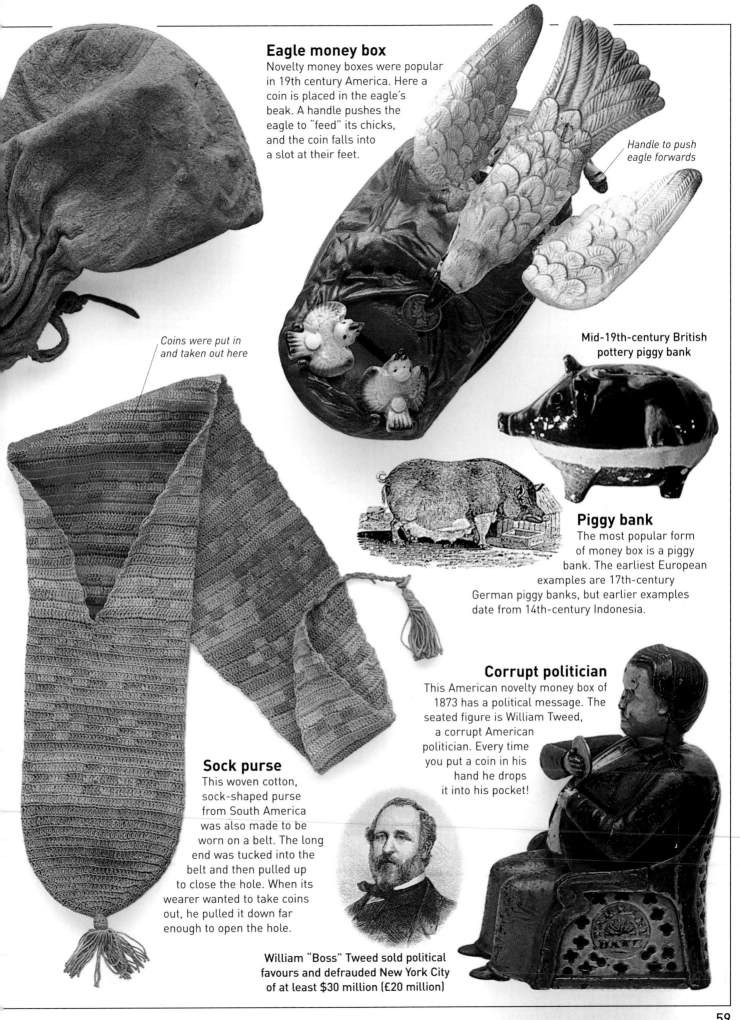

Eagle money box

Novelty money boxes were popular in 19th century America. Here a coin is placed in the eagle's beak. A handle pushes the eagle to "feed" its chicks, and the coin falls into a slot at their feet.

Handle to push eagle forwards

Coins were put in and taken out here

Mid-19th-century British pottery piggy bank

Piggy bank

The most popular form of money box is a piggy bank. The earliest European examples are 17th-century German piggy banks, but earlier examples date from 14th-century Indonesia.

Corrupt politician

This American novelty money box of 1873 has a political message. The seated figure is William Tweed, a corrupt American politician. Every time you put a coin in his hand he drops it into his pocket!

Sock purse

This woven cotton, sock-shaped purse from South America was also made to be worn on a belt. The long end was tucked into the belt and then pulled up to close the hole. When its wearer wanted to take coins out, he pulled it down far enough to open the hole.

William "Boss" Tweed sold political favours and defrauded New York City of at least $30 million (£20 million)

Cheques and plastic

Most of today's money cannot be put in a pocket because it exists only as electronic data in bank and business computers. Some will be changed into cash before it is used, but most will pay into another computer. Before computers, money was held in written records, and payments were made by hand on printed forms called cheques. In recent decades, plastic cards have replaced them.

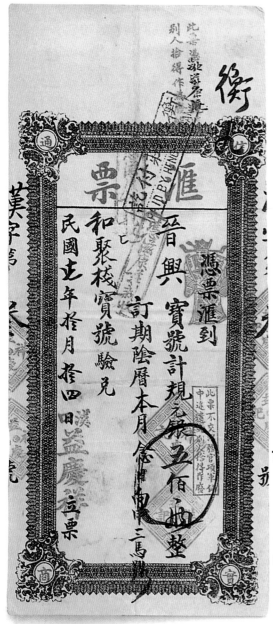

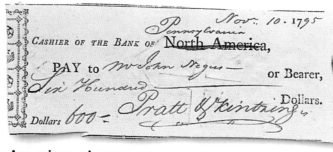

American cheque
This cheque instructs a bank to pay 600 dollars to a Mr. John Negus, or to anyone he gave the cheque to – in other words, the Bearer.

Travel money
Traveller's cheques were used by people going abroad. They bought cheques from a bank and changed them into foreign currency at their destination.

Chinese bill
500 ounces of silver had to be paid out on the order of this bill issued in 1928 by the Yi-qing-xiang Bank of Hankou, Central China.

Money order
A French candy store used this money order to pay a supplier 13 francs and 20 centimes for the goods received.

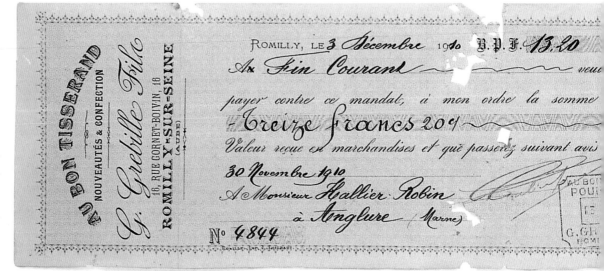

Telephone cards

These cards represent money already paid, the value of which is deducted from the card when a call is made from a public phone.

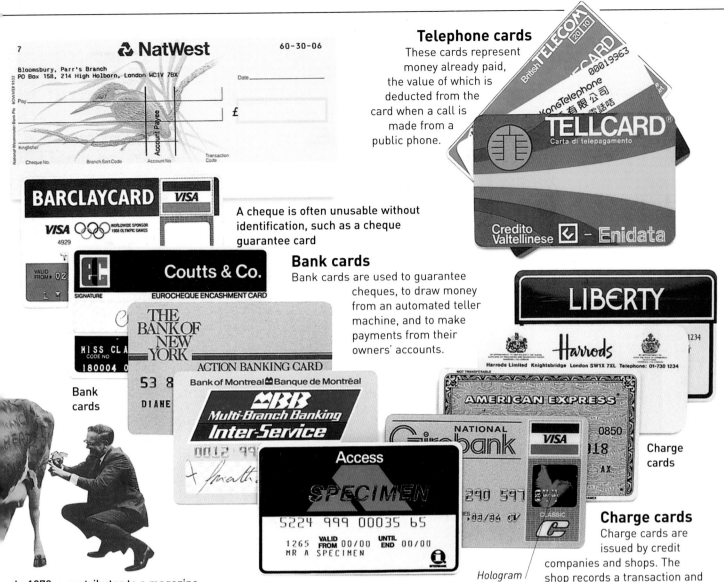

A cheque is often unusable without identification, such as a cheque guarantee card

Bank cards

Bank cards are used to guarantee cheques, to draw money from an automated teller machine, and to make payments from their owners' accounts.

Bank cards

SPECIMEN

In 1970, a contributor to a magazine received his payment in the form of a cheque written on a cow!

Hologram

Charge cards

Charge cards

Charge cards are issued by credit companies and shops. The shop records a transaction and the intention of the cardholder to pay; the bill must be paid later with cash or by cheque.

Embedded microchip acts as a built-in computer

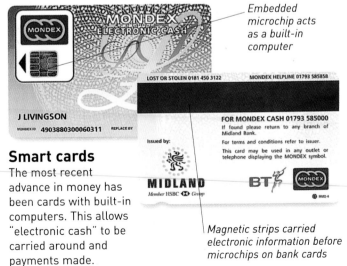

Smart cards

The most recent advance in money has been cards with built-in computers. This allows "electronic cash" to be carried around and payments made.

Magnetic strips carried electronic information before microchips on bank cards

Electronic cash

The development of computers and the introduction of the Internet has revolutionized money. Much of the world's money exists only as electronic records, and huge sums can be passed through the Internet.

ATM banking

Automated teller machines (ATMs) have changed the way that people use their local bank. The ATM is a bank counter that is always open, giving customers all the services they need through a computer interface.

Collecting coins

Coin designs and inscriptions provide a fascinating view of world history. They reveal things about the emperors, kings, and queens who issued them, and the traders and ordinary people who used them. Anyone can make their own collection, and one of the best ways is by theme, such as horses, boats, and birds.

Saved for posterity
Many coins now owned by collectors were once buried for safety. Luckily for the collectors, their owners were unable, or forgot, to recover them.

A soft toothbrush will not damage your coins

Rubbing alcohol

Rubbing alcohol
The best way to clean coins is to wipe them with cotton balls dipped in rubbing alcohol – ask an adult to help.

Cotton balls

Paper envelopes
As paper envelopes do not contain corrosive acid, they do not damage coins. Notes can also be written on envelopes.

A toothpick will get most dirt off without scratching, and a pen cap is good for getting coins out of the tray

Looking after your coins
As old coins have been handled by lots of people, and perhaps even spent time buried in the ground, they are often dirty. Clean them with rubbing alcohol, soap, or detergent first, and dry them thoroughly. If the dirt is stubborn, use a soft toothbrush or a piece of soft wood. If that does not work, seek advice from an experienced coin collector.

A metal point can be used with care

A magnifying glass is essential to see the fine details of coin designs

What not to do

Keeping your coins clean and safely stored will make them nicer to look at and safe from corrosion. Never use metal polish or a wire brush to clean coins – you will clean the designs right off them! Never store your coins in plastic envelopes; they may look nice when they are new, but after a while they get sticky and will ruin your coins. Never put your sticky fingers anywhere near coins as this makes them dirty.

Sticky fingers have made this coin dirty

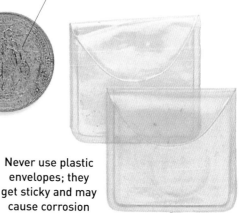

Never use plastic envelopes; they get sticky and may cause corrosion

A plastic envelope caused the green corrosion on this coin

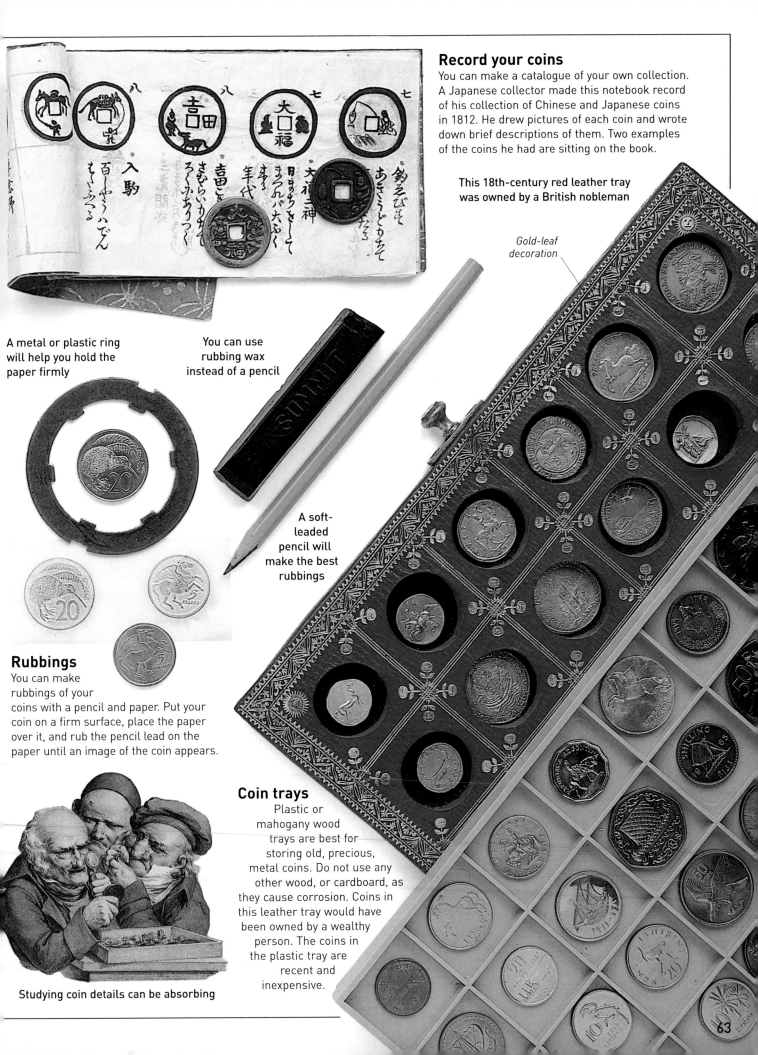

Record your coins

You can make a catalogue of your own collection. A Japanese collector made this notebook record of his collection of Chinese and Japanese coins in 1812. He drew pictures of each coin and wrote down brief descriptions of them. Two examples of the coins he had are sitting on the book.

This 18th-century red leather tray was owned by a British nobleman

Gold-leaf decoration

A metal or plastic ring will help you hold the paper firmly

You can use rubbing wax instead of a pencil

A soft-leaded pencil will make the best rubbings

Rubbings

You can make rubbings of your coins with a pencil and paper. Put your coin on a firm surface, place the paper over it, and rub the pencil lead on the paper until an image of the coin appears.

Coin trays

Plastic or mahogany wood trays are best for storing old, precious, metal coins. Do not use any other wood, or cardboard, as they cause corrosion. Coins in this leather tray would have been owned by a wealthy person. The coins in the plastic tray are recent and inexpensive.

Studying coin details can be absorbing

AMAZING FACTS

Counterfeiting was around long before paper money. In colonial America, purple wampum beads made of quahog clam shells were twice as valuable as white beads of whelk shells. Some people painted white beads purple to make more profit.

Quahog clam shell

One of the first coins to be minted in the United States was the 1792 half disme. A total of 1,500 half-dismes were produced by official mint personnel, before an actual mint was built. The coins were made in the cellar of a building at Sixth and Cherry Streets in Washington, DC. Legend goes that some were coined from Martha Washington's silverware.

George Washington did not appear on the first US coins, which portrayed icons such as Lady Liberty and the bald eagle. He did not appear on a coin until the 1899 commemorative "Lafayette Dollar", which featured portraits of both Washington and the Marquis de Lafayette. In 1932, his face was first featured on the quarter.

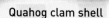

Buffalo Nickel

Metal money was originally exchanged in lumps or bars. A bigger lump was worth more, and for every transaction, the lump had to be carefully weighed to determine the value. The word "spend" comes from the Latin word *expendere*, meaning to weigh out.

Before coins were made by machines, some people shaved off their edges to obtain precious metal, an act called clipping. Clippings could be melted down and sold. To stop this practice, ridges were put around the edges of coins.

Gold is not the only treasure at the US Bullion Depository at Fort Knox, Kentucky. In World War II, the original copies of the Declaration of Independence, the Constitution, and the Bill of Rights were secretly stored there. The British Magna Carta and Crown Jewels, and the crown, sword, and sceptre of St Stephen, King of Hungary, were also stored there.

The crown, sceptre, and sword of the Hungarian king

The Buffalo Nickel, circulated in America between 1913 and 1938, features an image of a majestic animal, ready to roam. But the model for the coin, a buffalo named Black Diamond, lived in the Central Park Zoo in New York City.

In 1988, Australia became the first nation to circulate plastic currency. Produced with a durable polymer material, plastic money lasts four times longer than paper money. More than 20 countries now have plastic notes.

The name for a piggy bank comes from *pygg*, a clay used in the Middle Ages to make pots for money. The idea to make banks in the shape of pigs probably came from the similarity of the words.

The "life expectancy" of a coin in circulation is 30 years. A small bill changes hands so often it must be replaced in two years, while a large bill lasts for 10 years.

The French word for wedge is *coigne*. The dies used to stamp metal into coins were wedge-shaped, so money was given the name *coin*.

The US Mint produces up to 20 billion coins a year. Mint marks (a tiny letter by the subject's face on the front of each coin) tell you where the coins came from: P for Philadelphia, or D for Denver.

The US Federal Reserve Bank in New York has the world's largest accumulation of gold: 13 million fine troy ounces (a fine troy ounce is a troy ounce of pure gold content in a gold bar; a troy ounce weighs 31.1 g). Only 2 per cent of the gold belongs to the US. The 63 "account holders" are 49 countries, and the rest are international organizations.

Bank is white ceramic with blue flowers

Piggy bank

QUESTIONS AND ANSWERS

Q How much money is in circulation in the United States?

A According to America's Federal Reserve, as of August 2015 there was about $1.3 trillion in US coins and bills in circulation. This amount has risen rapidly in recent years, due to increasing demand from abroad.

Q How does new currency enter circulation?

A While most people cash a cheque or go to an ATM cash machine, American banks get cash from 12 regional Federal Reserve Banks. Most banks have reserve accounts with the Fed. They pay for the cash they get by having money deducted from those accounts. Most countries have central banks that operate in the same way.

Q How many currencies are there?

A Most countries have their own currencies, but some African nations and Caribbean islands share a currency. There are 180 different currencies in use today. A currency is considered to be in use is if it is traded on the exchange market.

Traders on the foreign exchange floor

Q What are some of the ways that paper bills are protected from counterfeiting?

A Security features prevent paper money from being reproduced easily. Many bills include watermarks, faint images that are only visible when the bill is held up to the light. Plastic security threads embedded in the paper glow under an ultraviolet light. Colour-shifting inks, whose colour looks different at different angles, are sometimes used, and the bill may also be printed all over with tiny words (called microprinting). Adding holograms or kinograms (images that change when tilted) to currency is the latest trend in anti-counterfeiting.

Q What happens to worn-out paper money?

A When US banks have an excess of cash on hand, they deposit it with the Federal Reserve Bank. The Fed checks the condition of notes to see if they can circulate again. About one-third of the notes are destroyed by shredding. Some shredded bills are recycled into products such as stationery. Any counterfeit bills are separated and sent for investigation. When the Federal Reserve needs new money, it orders it from the Bureau of Engraving and Printing.

Q What is the foreign exchange market?

A The value of one currency compared to another is called the exchange rate. The rate is determined at the foreign exchange markets of cities like New York, London, Tokyo, and Paris, where dealers buy and sell currency of different countries. The rate fluctuates every minute of every day, depending on supply and demand.

Holograms used to combat counterfeiting

Q How is money exchanged on the Internet today?

A The Internet is a new way to exchange money. Most online purchases are made with credit cards, but clearing houses have been set up so people can send and receive payments in different currencies.

Record Breakers

LARGEST GOLD COIN:
A 1,012-kg (2,231-lb) coin crafted in 2012 by Perth Mint, Australia, with a legal value of $1 million. The coin features the image of Queen Elizabeth II, head of state, on one side, and a leaping kangaroo on the other. It is one tonne of 99.99 per cent pure gold.

MOST VALUABLE COIN:
A 1794 Flowing Hair silver dollar sold for a record $10 million at an auction in 2013.

WORLD'S LARGEST BANK NOTE:
In 1998, to mark the Centennial of Philippine independence from Spanish rule, the government issued a giant bank note, measuring 22 x 33 cm (8.5 x 13 in).

WORLD'S SMALLEST BANK NOTE:
A 1917 Romanian note measured 2.75 x 3.8 cm (1.49 x 1.08 in) – about the size of a postage stamp.

Timeline of banking

The story of money is also told through the way people store money: banking. A bank is a financial institution where people keep their money safe. Banks extend credit to their customers. The word "bank" comes from the Italian word for bench, *banca*. Italian money lenders made transactions from park benches.

European knights on crusade

c.3000 BCE The roots of banking emerge in Mesopotamia, as temples and palaces are used for "deposits" of grain and other valuables. Eventually, private houses were also set up for the same purpose.

c.1792–1750 BCE Under the reign of Hammurabi, King of Babylon, a set of laws called the Code of Hammurabi is issued. The Code includes laws to govern banking.

c.600 BCE The first mention of a merchant banker in the ancient world. The banker, named Pythius, trades throughout Asia Minor.

c.394 BCE A slave in Athens named Pasion becomes the city's wealthiest banker. He gains citizenship after giving money to the state.

King Hammurabi

390 BCE The Gauls launch a surprise attack on the Capitoline Hill in Rome, where the city's money reserves are kept. Geese alert Roman soldiers, and the invasion is foiled. The Romans build a shrine on the hill to Moneta, goddess of warning; her name gives the words for money and mint.

323 BCE State granaries work as banks in Egypt. Payments are transferred without money changing hands.

c.900 CE The Chinese government issues paper money. Its use is widespread for the next 500 years, until the Mongol conquest.

1095–1270 The Europeans launch Crusades to reclaim the Holy Lands of the Middle East. The need to transfer money for troops and supplies gives a boost to new European banking.

1171 The Bank of Venice is founded in Italy to loan money to the government.

1400s–1600s The Medici family, based in Florence, Italy, become leading figures in the Renaissance era. Their enormous wealth was acquired largely through banking.

1401 The Bank of Barcelona is founded in Barcelona, Spain. This bank is considered to be the first to offer basic banking operations. For example, the bank held deposits, exchanged currency, and lent money.

1450s The Fuggers, a German banking family, reach their peak. They dominate European banking until the royal houses of France and Spain default on loans and the bank goes under.

1545 Britain's King Henry VIII legalizes interest rates on loans, but sets an upper limit of 10 per cent per year. His legislation is annulled by Parliament under King Edward VI in 1552.

1566 The Royal Exchange is founded in England for London to become a financial power.

1609 The Bank of Amsterdam is founded in Holland. It is set up to receive gold and silver deposits.

1619 The Hamburg Girobank is founded in Germany. It is Germany's first commercial bank, and lasts until its takeover by the state-run Reichsbank in 1875.

1630s British goldsmiths, who sometimes deal in coins and let customers use their safes for depositing gold and other valuables, evolve into bankers.

1659 A British cheque is issued for 400 pounds sterling. It is the oldest existing cheque.

1668 Sveriges Riksbank (the Bank of Sweden) is founded in Stockholm. It is the world's first central bank.

1660 With a shortage of silver coins, the Stockholm Bank of Sweden issues Europe's first printed paper money.

1694 The Banks of England and Scotland are founded to serve the English and Scottish governments.

1716 The first public bank in France, the Banque Generale, opens to customers.

1728 The Royal Bank of Scotland introduces a system in which certain people are given a line of credit against future deposits; this is the origin of the overdraft.

Catherine the Great

1768 The first banks are established in Russia. They are created by Catherine the Great to help finance Russia's war with the Ottoman Empire (present-day Turkey). The bank issued paper currency the next year.

66

1772 Scotland establishes eight bank branches throughout the country, making it the first country in the world to establish a nationwide system of branch banking.

1780 The Bank of Pennsylvania is founded to raise money for the Continental Army. It is the first American bank since the Declaration of Independence.

The Bank of Pennsylvania

1791 The First Bank of the United States is formed in an early attempt to centralize America's banking system. It becomes the country's largest corporation, but its charter is not renewed in 1811 because Americans are uncomfortable with the existence of one all-powerful bank.

1803 The Louisiana Purchase (doubling the size of the United States) is funded through loans to the US government from two British banks. French leader Napoleon sells the land to the US for $15 million.

1816 Members of the Rothschild family, a dynasty of German Jewish bankers, are made barons.

1836–1865 The USA enters the Free Banking Era. Almost anyone can print money – from a restaurant to a railway company. There are as many as 8,000 different issuers of money during this era, and counterfeits are almost impossible to detect.

1864 With Abraham Lincoln's support, the National Bank Act in the United States ends the Free Banking Era by providing a national currency.

1865 The Latin Monetary Union is established in France, with members including Belgium, Italy, Switzerland, and Greece. Members kept their own currency name and coin design, but used a common standard of currency.

1881 Postal orders (money orders purchased at the post office) are introduced in Britain.

1914 The US Federal Reserve system is established with 12 regional banks.

1929, 24 October The Great Crash of the New York Stock Exchange.

1929–1933 The Great Depression. The failure of banks is widespread, and remaining banks cut back on lending, so people and businesses go bankrupt.

1933 The Federal Deposit Insurance Corporation (FDIC) is created in the United States to insure bank deposits.

1950 The first American drive-through banking window opens in Columbus, Ohio.

1969 The International Monetary Fund (IMF) creates the Special Drawing Rate; participating countries can draw funds from reserves in times of crisis.

1972 A patent for the automatic teller machine (ATM) is issued to Don Wetzel.

1978 SMART cards, patented in 1974 by Roland Moreno, the inventor of the microchip, are mass produced for the first time.

1979 The European Monetary System is created to link the currencies of the European Union.

Newspaper announcing the great stock-market crash of 24 October 1929

1988 The savings-and-loan crisis peaks in the USA. Hundreds of savings-and-loan associations go under, costing the federal fund that insures them billions of dollars.

1999 The euro is introduced into the countries belonging to the European Union. By 2002, euro bank notes and coins replace the former national currencies in member states.

2005 A major survey shows banking is the fastest-growing Internet activity.

2007 Start of the 21st-century financial crisis, bringing a credit crunch that results in the failure and bail-out of many of the world's biggest banks.

US and French representatives exchange documents in the Louisiana Purchase

Find out more

If you want to find out more about money, there is a wealth of opportunities. Pay a visit to places where paper notes are printed and coins are created. Touring these facilities reveals the history of money, and gives you a chance to see a fortune in new cash on the production line. If you live near a city with a central bank, check for tour information on the Internet. In the USA, branches of the Federal Reserve Bank have historical museums and free tours to explain banking. Consider opening a savings account at your local bank. You could start a coin collection by looking online for information about local coin shows or coin clubs.

Money museum
Many museums have collections of coins and paper money, allowing visitors to view rare and ancient forms of currency, such as these two beautiful decadrachms from the ancient Greek colony of Syracuse.

Start a coin collection
Starting your own coin or paper money collection can be a great hobby. There are plenty of magazines, books, and websites devoted to collecting. You could also look for a rare-coin dealer in your area, and ask his or her advice on the best way to get started.

USEFUL WEBSITES

www.money.org
Explore the world of money on the home page of the American Numismatic Association.

www.usmint.gov/kids/
The Internet home of the US Mint.

www.moneyfactory.com
A fun site from the Bureau of Engraving and Printing teaching about money in the USA.

www.fdic.gov/about/learn/learning/
A kid's guide to the FDIC and banking.

www.federalreserveeducation.org
An interactive guide to the Federal Reserve system reveals the life of a cheque or dollar bill.

A tonne of gold bricks

Tour the vault of the Federal Reserve Bank in New York City, USA, and you will see one-third of all the world's monetary gold! It is kept in special "cages", one for each nation's central bank. When one country sells gold to another, it is moved between cages by workers wearing shoe covers to protect their feet from dropped bricks.

Attend a coin show

Coin shows, at which dealers show and sell their collections, are frequently scheduled on weekends across the country. You'll be able to chat with the dealers and see amazing coins.

Savings account

An important part of learning about money is finding out how to keep it. Setting up your own savings account is the first step to financial responsibility. Many banks offer free savings accounts for children under a specified age. Most banks will accept a low deposit and you will earn interest on the money saved.

Minting of a 2004 nickel marking the Louisiana Purchase

The Royal Canadian Mint, Ottawa, Ontario

This tool rotates as it polishes each coin

This is the die from which the special nickels are stamped

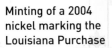

Where money comes from

The notes and change in your pocket were printed or minted. Check the Internet and find out where your currency is made. In the USA, paper money is printed at the Federal Bureau of Engraving and Printing in Washington, DC. Coins are made in both the Denver and Philadelphia branches of the US Mint.

PLACES TO VISIT

UNITED STATES MINT PHILADELPHIA, PA, AND DENVER, CO

Tours cover the history of the Mint and all stages of the minting process, from creating the original design to striking the coins.

BUREAU OF ENGRAVING AND PRINTING, WASHINGTON, DC, AND FORT WORTH, TX

Watch millions of dollars being printed right before your eyes at these two facilities, and learn all about the production of currency.

MUSEUM OF AMERICAN FINANCIAL HISTORY, NEW YORK, NY

This museum explores significant events in US history from a financial perspective.

MONEY MUSEUM, COLORADO SPRINGS, CO

America's largest museum dedicated to numismatics consists of 400,000 objects.

FEDERAL RESERVE BANK OF NEW YORK, NY

Feast your eyes on a small portion of the world's largest cache of gold.

FEDERAL RESERVE BANK OF CLEVELAND, OH

Take a first-hand look at the Fed's cash-processing operation on this tour.

FEDERAL RESERVE BANK OF CHICAGO, CHICAGO, IL

See what a million dollars looks like, and try your skill at detecting counterfeit bills.

NATIONAL NUMISMATIC COLLECTION, SMITHSONIAN INSTITUTION, WASHINGTON, DC

This is one of the most important collections in the world, with 1.6 million objects.

Glossary

ALLOY
A mixture containing two or more elements, at least one of which is metallic, fused together.

ASSIGNATS
Treasury notes issued during the French Revolution to redeem the huge public debt.

French assignat, 1793

BANK NOTE
A bill or piece of paper money, especially one issued by a nation's central bank. Bank notes are usually printed on paper or plastic.

BARTER
A trade in which goods or services are exchanged directly for other goods and services, without the use of money. Barter is the oldest form of trade, and remains an important means of trade for countries using currencies that are not readily convertible on world currency exchange markets.

BILL OF EXCHANGE
An unconditional payment demand for a specific sum of money, payable either at once or at a specified future date. A bill of exchange is drawn up by the seller and presented to the buyer.

BLANKS
A featureless circle of metal onto which a coin's design is minted, or marked.

BULLION
Bars or ingots of precious metals, usually in standardized sizes.

CACAO BEAN
A bean that grows inside large pods on the cacao tree. Cacao beans make cocoa and chocolate, and were currency in Pre-Columbian Mexico.

CARAT
A measure of the purity of gold. Pure gold is 24 carats.

CIRCULATION
The spread or transmission of money to a group or area.

COIN CLIPPING
The practice of trimming small shavings from the edges of coins made from pure metals, and melting them down for sale. The clipping was so minimal that coins could still be used as currency.

COLOUR PROOF
In bank note production, a representation of the final printed product, used to check accuracy.

COMMEMORATIVE COINS
A special coin featuring a design honouring a person, place, or event.

Cowrie shells

Holder for cowrie shells

COMMODITY
Any raw material, such as wheat, silver, soybeans, or livestock. When people buy commodities, they hope the price will rise, so they can sell at a profit.

COWRIE
Any of many tropical marine gastropods with highly polished shells, which are used as currency in India, Africa, and Thailand.

CUNEIFORM
A system of writing in the ancient Near East, and perhaps the earliest writing system. Cuneiform writers used tools to make characters on wet clay tablets, which were later fired to harden and preserve them.

CUPRO-NICKEL
An alloy made of approximately 75 per cent copper and 25 per cent nickel, widely used all over the world for coinage because of its long-lasting properties and low production cost.

CURRENCY
A country's official unit of monetary exchange; the metal or paper money issued by the government.

DENOMINATION
The face value of a coin or bank note in the currency of the issuing country. The denomination is usually stamped or printed on the coin or bank note itself.

DIE
A device used for shaping metal; for example, in minting coins.

DISME
The original spelling of "dime", or one-tenth of a dollar. This term was in widespread use in the 17th century.

Minting die

DOUBLOON
An early Spanish gold coin.

DRACHMA
A silver coin used in ancient Greece.

DUCAT
A gold coin once in use in several European countries.

ELECTRUM
A naturally occurring alloy of silver and gold. Electrum was used to make some of the world's first coins.

EURO
A common currency that has replaced the individual currencies of most countries in the European Union.

EXPORT
Any goods or services sold abroad. It can describe the shipment or transfer of goods and services out of a country.

FLORIN
A unit of currency formerly used in the Netherlands and other parts of Europe.

FORGERY
The process of making or changing objects or documents with the intention to deceive someone.

GOLD DUST
The particles and flakes of gold obtained by mining.

GREENBACKS
A nickname for American dollars, originally used to describe the bank notes issued by the US government during the Civil War.

HIEROGLYPHICS
A system of writing in which the characters are pictures of objects, animals, or human beings.

HOLEY DOLLAR
A coin with a hole in the centre, the official currency of New South Wales, Australia, from 1813 to 1822.

Holey dollar

INGOT
A mass of metal, such as gold, cast in a mould to give it a convenient shape (usually a block or bar) for storage or transportation. Ingots are later re-melted so the metal can be cast or rolled.

INTAGLIO
A type of printmaking in which an image is etched onto a metal plate. Ink is then applied to the etched areas beneath the plate's surface. When pressed against damp paper, the inked plate prints the image in reverse.

LETTERPRESS
A printing method that stamps ink onto paper from a raised surface.

LITHOGRAPHY
A printing process based on the fact that water and oil will not mix together.

MANILLA
In West Africa, a copper ring used from the 15th century.

MINT
The official government building at which coins are struck, or minted.

MINTING
The process of forming coins by stamping, punching, or printing. The process of minting – stamping a design onto metal by pressing it between two hard metal dies – was invented 2,600 years ago in Lydia (Turkey).

MISER
A stingy person who hoards money and possessions and lives frugally.

MONETARY UNION
The result of two or more governments deciding to share a common currency.

MONEY ORDER
A cheque that a customer can buy from a post office or financial institution, issued to a payee for a specific amount.

OWL COINS
Silver coins issued in ancient Greece featuring the image of an owl, considered a special bird. Greeks traded internationally with these coins.

PESO
A silver coin used in the Spanish colonies of the Americas, and a modern currency in some countries.

PIECE OF EIGHT
An old Spanish coin worth eight reales.

PLATE MONEY
Huge, heavy copper coins once issued in Sweden. Many coins weighed 2 kg (4 pounds).

Greek owl coin

PUNCH
A tool used to make holes in minting.

SECURITY THREAD
A metallic or polyester strip embedded in a bank note paper. Bills featuring a security thread are very difficult to forge.

Manillas made of copper

Manillas

SCISSEL
The metal strip left behind after coins are stamped.

SIEGE MONEY
Currency issued at various times in history when a city was cut off by a siege. It paid for soldiers and necessities when official currency ran out.

SMART CARD
A card that contains a computer chip, and stores or processes information.

TOKEN
A metal or plastic disc used as a coin substitute to redeem a product or service.

Marks on a touchstone

TOUCHSTONE
A black stone used to test the quality (in carats) of a gold coin. A trader would rub the coin against the stone, then compare the streak left to a set of thin gold needles of various carats.

TRADE
The exchange of goods and services; all the buying and selling that takes place in domestic and foreign markets.

UPSETTING MILL
In coin minting, a rotating wheel with a groove to create a rim on both sides.

WAMPUM
Small beads made from polished clam shells and fashioned into strings or belts. Wampum was used by American Indian tribes as money and jewellery.

WATERMARK
A design embossed into paper during its production. The watermark is seen when the paper is held up to the light. This is one way for bank note printers to prevent counterfeit paper money.

Index

Acknowledgments

The publisher and the author would like to thank:
Thomas Keenes for additional design assistance; Peter Hayman (pp.58–59), Karl Shone pp.26–27), Kate Warren (pp.8–9) for special photography; the staff of the British Museum who helped, particularly Janet Larkin, Suzie Chan, Virginia Hewitt, Andy Meadows, Sue Crundwell, Brendan Moore, and Keith Howes of the Coins and Medals Department; Travellers Exchange Corporation plc for the supply of international currencies; The Museum of Mankind; The Royal Mint; De La Rue; HSBC; European Monetary Institute; The National Westminster Bank; Pollock's Toy Museum; The National Philatelic Society; The Hungarian International Bank; G Smith & Sons; Sothebys of London; Dr Fergus Duncan; Coin Craft; Kiwi Fruits, London; Barclays Bank Ltd; Robert Tye; Steve Cribb; Bill Barrett; Howard Simmons; Andrew Oddy; Clare Nelson; Graham Dyer; Kevin Clancy; Edwin Green; Margaret, Laurence,

Dunstan, Althea and Ruth Cribb; James Taylor; Anna and Katie Martin; Jane Parker for the index; Andrea Mills for text editing and Polly Goodman for proofreading.

The publisher would like to thank the following for their kind permission to reproduce their images:

Picture credits:
(t=top, b=bottom, c=centre, l=left, r=right)

AKG Photo: 28m
Aldus Archive: 22bl, 37tr, 51c
Ancient Art & Architecture Collection: 6bc
The British Library: 60t
The British Museum: 7tl, 17, 40c, 46c, 60b
Burgerbibliothek, Bern: 32c
J. Allan Cash Photolibrary: 8br, 36cr, 56cl
Dennis R. Cooper: 30t
E.T. Archive: 34bl, 52c
Mary Evans Picture Library: 8tl, 22c,

24tl, 24bl, 25t, 25cl, 31r, 35cl, 36tc, 38b, 39tl, 42tl, 46b, 50, 53c, 56tr
Fotomas Index: 21tl
Robert Harding Picture Library: 29bc, 30b, 38tl
Michael Holford: 11cr, 46tl
Hulton-Deutsch: 33tr, 57b
Hutchison Library: 52tl
Mansell Collection: 13c, 40tl, 42bl
National Portrait Gallery, London: 34cr
Peter Newark's Pictures: 28tl, 48, 49
Pollock's Toy Museum, London: 56b
Popperfoto: 29cr, 41br
Punch: 58–59c
Louvre/c. Réunion des Musées Nationaux: 34tl
The Royal Mint: 14–15
Spectrum Colour Library: 41l
Worthing Museum & Art Gallery: 57cr
Zefa: 12cr, 27tr, 28bl, 42cr, 59bc

American Numismatic Association: 69tl
AP Wideworld: 65br
Aziz Khan: 29tr
Bridgeman Art Library: Louvre, Paris, France 66cl;
Private Collection, Archives Charmet 66tr
Corbis: 67tl; Archivo Iconografico, S.A. 66br; Craig Aumess 69tr; Bettmann

67bl; Yves Forestier 65tr; Wolfgang Kaehler 64tr; Lee Snider 68br; Joseph Sohm; ChromoSohm Inc. 64–65
DK: Chas Howson/British Museum 70tl, 71cr, 71cl; Nick Nicholls/British Museum 71bl; David Garner/Exeter Museum 71tr; Dave King/Pitt Rivers Museum 70bl; Science Museum London 70br; Yorkshire Museum 70cr
Getty Images: 67cr, 69bc; AFP 65bl
Smithsonian Museum of American History: 68tl
US Mint Image: 64cl

Illustrators: Thomas Keenes: 10c, 20c, 54t and b, 55t and b; Kathleen McDougall: 12t, 32t; John Woodcock: 29tr

Picture Research: Kathy Lockley; Frances Vargo

The objects on the following pages are smaller than their actual size: pp6–7; 8–9; 12–13; 14–15; 26–27; 58–59; 60–61; 62–63. All current bank notes are reproduced at a reduced size, and in some cases in black and white, according to the reproduction regulations of the country concerned.

All other images © Dorling Kindersley
For further information see: www.dkimages.com